STUDENT DISCIPLINE

A GUIDE TO THE EDUCATION AMENDMENT ACT, 2007

SECOND EDITION

Jennifer E. Trépanier
Shibley Righton LLP

Student Discipline: A Guide to the Education Amendment Act, 2007, Second Edition
© LexisNexis Canada Inc. 2008
April 2008

All rights reserved. No part of this publication may be reproduced, stored in any material form (including photocopying or storing it in any medium by electronic means and whether or not transiently or incidentally to some other use of this publication) without the written permission of the copyright holder except in accordance with the provisions of the Copyright Act. Applications for the copyright holder's written permission to reproduce any part of this publication should be addressed to the publisher.

Warning: The doing of an unauthorized act in relation to a copyrighted work may result in both a civil claim for damages and criminal prosecution.

Members of the LexisNexis Group worldwide

Canada	LexisNexis Canada Inc, 123 Commerce Valley Dr. E. Suite 700, MARKHAM, Ontario
Argentina	Abeledo Perrot, Jurisprudencia Argentina and Depalma, BUENOS AIRES
Australia	Butterworths, a Division of Reed International Books Australia Pty Ltd, CHATSWOOD, New South Wales
Austria	ARD Betriebsdienst and Verlag Orac, VIENNA
Chile	Publitecsa and Conosur Ltda, SANTIAGO DE CHILE
Czech Republic	Orac, sro, PRAGUE
France	Éditions du Juris-Classeur SA, PARIS
Hong Kong	Butterworths Asia (Hong Kong), HONG KONG
Hungary	Hvg Orac, BUDAPEST
India	Butterworths India, NEW DELHI
Ireland	Butterworths (Ireland) Ltd, DUBLIN
Italy	Giuffré, MILAN
Malaysia	Malayan Law Journal Sdn Bhd, KUALA LUMPUR
New Zealand	Butterworths of New Zealand, WELLINGTON
Poland	Wydawnictwa Prawnicze PWN, WARSAW
Singapore	Butterworths Asia, SINGAPORE
South Africa	Butterworth Publishers (Pty) Ltd, DURBAN
Switzerland	Stämpfli Verlag AG, BERNE
United Kingdom	Butterworths Tolley, a Division of Reed Elsevier (UK), LONDON, WC2A
USA	LexisNexis, DAYTON, Ohio

Library and Archives Canada Cataloguing in Publication

Trépanier, Jennifer E.
    Student discipline : a guide to the Education Amendment Act, 2007 / Jennifer E. Trépanier. — 2nd ed.

Includes index.
ISBN 978-0-433-45943-9

  1. Ontario. Safe Schools Act. 2. School discipline—Law and legislation—Ontario. I. Title.

KEO771.4.T74 2008   344.713'0793   C2008-905233-8
KF4124.5.T74 2008

Printed and bound in Canada.

To my husband for his support and encouragement,
to our children for their energy and affection,
and to my family, friends, and colleagues
for their support and friendship over the years.

A special thanks to my wonderful grandparents who allow us
to enjoy the rarity of four generations simultaneously.

About the Author

Jennifer Trépanier is a member of the Education and Public Law Group at Shibley Righton LLP. Raised in a family of educators, Jennifer is a natural fit in the Education Law field. She completed her law degree at the University of Western Ontario after receiving a master's degree in French language and literature.

Within the Education Law field, Jennifer's practice involves dealing with a range of issues including matters of student discipline, teacher misconduct, human rights, special education, labour and employment law, and litigation involving school boards or educational institutions. She has practised before various courts and administrative tribunals. Jennifer has also handled various matters involving French-language education issues, allowing her to utilize her French-language skills.

Former editor of the Shibley Righton Education Law NetLetter, published by LexisNexis Butterworths and a contributor to the Shibley Righton LLP Education Law eBulletin, Jennifer has written and presented papers on education law issues to a variety of audiences. Her articles have appeared in publications such as the Education and Law Journal, Education Canada, the Ontario Bar Association Education Law Newsletter and CAPSLE Comments (the publication of the Canadian Association for the Practical Study of Law in Education). Jennifer has given guest lectures and has provided instructional training on education law issues to a variety of audiences including teaching candidates, law students, administrators, administrators-in-training, educators and lawyers.

This text is intended to provide practical, "hands-on" advice to all of those educators who go to great lengths on a regular basis to maintain a safe school environment.

TABLE OF CONTENTS

About the Author v

COMMENTARY 1

A. INTRODUCTION 3
B. OVERVIEW OF CHANGES TO THE
   STUDENT DISCIPLINE REGIME 4
   1. No more "Mandatory Discipline" 4
   2. Mitigating Factors and Progressive Discipline 5
   3. Bullying and Off-School Property Conduct 5
   4. No more Teacher Suspensions 6
   5. No More Principal Expulsions 6
   6. Revisions to Time periods and Composition
      of Discipline Committees 7
   7. Education for Suspended and Expelled Pupils 7
   8. Code of Conduct 7
C. THE APPLICATION OF MITIGATING FACTORS
   AND PROGRESSIVE DISCIPLINE 8
   1. Mitigating and Other Factors 8
      (a) Overview 8
      (b) Application of the Factors 9
      (c) Application of the Factors to Pupils with Special Needs 10
   2. Progressive Discipline 11
      (a) Definition of Progressive Discipline 12
      (b) Progressive Discipline Policies 12
      (c) Progressive Discipline involving Students
          with Special Needs 14
D. SUSPENSIONS 15
   1. Overview 15
   2. Interpretation of Listed Activities 16
   3. Addition of "Bullying" 16
      (a) Definition of Bullying 16
      (b) Positive School Climate 18
      (c) School Board Policies on Bullying 18
   4. Off-School Property Conduct 20
   5. Mitigating and Other Factors 21
   6. Duration 21
   7. Completion of Forms 22
   8. Notice of Suspension 22
   9. Suspension Appeal Process 23
      (a) Who may Appeal? 23
      (b) Notice of Appeal 23

		(c)	Optional Review Process 23
		(d)	Suspension Appeal Hearing Process 23
		(e)	Parties to the Suspension Appeal 24
		(f)	Pupil's Right to Attend...24
		(g)	Powers of Board Committee 25
E.	EXPULSIONS...25
	1.	Overview 25
	2.	Duration of Suspension Leading to Possible Expulsion 26
	3.	Education for Pupils Suspended Pending Possible Expulsion 27
	4.	Notice of Suspension 27
	5.	Investigation 28
	6.	General Tips for Conducting Investigations 29
	7.	Mitigating or Other Factors 30
	8.	Steps to Follow Where Expulsion is Not Recommended 30
		(a)	Review of Initial Suspension..30
		(b)	Written Notice 30
		(c)	Appeal of Initial Suspension 31
	9.	Steps to Follow where Expulsion is Recommended 31
		(a)	Report regarding Recommendation..31
		(b)	Written Notice 32
		(c)	Response to Report 32
		(d)	Expulsion Hearing..33
		(e)	Board Committee Requirements 33
		(f)	Parties to an Expulsion Hearing 33
		(g)	Submissions at Expulsion Hearing..34
		(h)	Decision of Board Committee 34
	10.	Steps to Follow where Pupil is not Expelled 34
		(a)	Board Committee to Hear Appeal of Initial Suspension 34
		(b)	Written Notice of Board Committee Decisions...........................35
	11.	Steps to Follow where Pupil is Expelled 35
		(a)	Assignment of Expelled Pupil..35
		(b)	Written Notice of Board Committee Decisions...........................35
	12.	Expulsion Appeal Process 36
		(a)	Who may Appeal?..36
		(b)	Notice of Appeal 36
		(c)	Parties to the Expulsion Appeal 37
		(d)	Hearing of Appeal 37
		(e)	Powers of Designated Tribunal 37
		(f)	Decision of Tribunal..38
		(g)	Ministry Regulations regarding Expulsion Appeals...................38
F.	EDUCATION FOR SUSPENDED AND EXPELLED PUPILS 39
	1.	Overview 39
	2.	Board Policies regarding Education Programs 39
	3.	Education of Pupils under Short-Term Suspension 40
	4.	Education of Pupils under Long-Term Suspension or Expulsion 40
	5.	Return to School after Completion of Program 41

G. TRANSITIONAL PROVISIONS 43
   1.   Limited Expulsions 43
   2.   Full Expulsions 43
H. DENIAL OF ACCESS PROVISIONS 43
   1.   Removal of Application to Pupils 44
   2.   Implications regarding Pupils with Special Needs 45
I. DISCIPLINE OF PUPILS WITH SPECIAL NEEDS 46

LEGISLATION 49

Education Act, Part XIII 51
Education Act, s. 265 (1) 75
Access to School Premises Regulation 79
Suspension and Expulsion of Pupils Regulation 81

APPENDIX 85

Appendix A: Policy/Program Memorandum No. 128 87
Appendix B: Policy/Program Memorandum No. 141 99
Appendix C: Policy/Program Memorandum No. 142 115
Appendix D: Policy/Program Memorandum No. 144 135
Appendix E: Policy/Program Memorandum No. 145 145
Appendix F: Summary of *S.J. v. Toronto Catholic District School Board* 159
Appendix G: Summary of *K.B. v. Toronto District School Board* 163

Index 165

COMMENTARY

A. INTRODUCTION

Maintaining a safe school environment is perhaps the most important of the many duties with which a principal is entrusted. It is only within a safe and secure learning environment that pupils may achieve their full potential and flourish. One of a principal's greatest challenges is to maintain a safe school in a manner that is consistent with the legal complexities of the student discipline regime.

This text provides insight into the practical and legal implications of the *Education Amendment Act, 2007*[1] (hereinafter the "EAA"), passed in June of 2007 to take effect on February 1, 2008, which replaces the controversial provisions of the *Safe Schools Act, 2000*[2] (hereinafter the "*Safe Schools Act*").

Several years after the *Safe Schools Act* became law, educators, school boards, and school communities have continued to struggle with the implementation of its complex provisions. The notions of "mandatory discipline" and "zero-tolerance" that were associated with this legislation resulted in significant confusion and conflict within school communities across Ontario. Although the application and understanding of these provisions has evolved over time, the conflicts engendered by the *Safe Schools Act* continue to be litigated through the courts today.

While the *Safe Schools Act* focussed on the discipline of students for specific conduct, the EAA focuses on a pro-active approach to preventing misconduct, and when misconduct does occur, addressing it with a progressive discipline approach that promotes positive behaviour through means that are corrective and supportive, rather than solely punitive.

It is hoped that the 2007 changes to the student discipline regime will be conducive to a more pro-active approach to matters of student discipline and that its implementation will be less challenging than its predecessor. That being said, although the EAA attempts to streamline the student discipline process, in some respects it imposes more detailed statutory requirements than previously existed. In addition, the EAA imposes some procedural requirements that may create practical difficulties for school boards when scheduling discipline proceedings. Further, the EAA removes various disciplinary powers of principals, instead placing more power in the hands of trustees, which may create difficulties for principals to maintain safe schools in situations involving serious safety concerns. It

---

[1] R.S.O. 1990, c. E.2.
[2] S.O. 2000, c. 12, s. 3.

remains to be seen how all of these factors will unfold in Ontario's school communities as the EAA is implemented.

This text highlights the changes to the student discipline regime implemented by the EAA and provides a framework to help navigate the legal complexities of the new regime.

The text is divided into the following parts: (1) COMMENTARY, which focuses on the legislative changes in the EAA and related regulations, (2) LEGISLATION, which includes excerpts of the relevant statutory provisions and regulations and (3) APPENDIX, which reproduces the Policy/Program Memoranda discussed in the Commentary and also provides a summary of two student discipline cases that address issues of school safety.

B. OVERVIEW OF CHANGES TO THE STUDENT DISCIPLINE REGIME

1. No more "Mandatory Discipline"

The amendments to the *Education Act*[3] (hereinafter "the *Education Act*") have removed the language of "mandatory" discipline and replaced it with language of discretionary discipline. In the writer's opinion, the notions of mandatory discipline and zero-tolerance (although widely misunderstood to be part of the Safe Schools Regime)[4] have not existed since Regulations 37/01 and 106/01[5] were passed which required principals to consider mitigating factors before imposing discipline.

In any event, it is now clear that principals have the discretion to decide whether to suspend, and that school boards have the discretion to decide whether to expel.

Although discipline is no longer labelled as mandatory, the general structure of the discipline process remains unchanged. Certain listed "activities", formerly referred to as "infractions" may result in discipline. As was previously the case, a principal is required to follow certain steps when considering the imposition of such discipline, and there are various levels of appeals provided in respect of student discipline decisions.

---

[3] R.S.O. 1990, c. E.2.
[4] The term "Safe Schools Regime" is used to describe the era when the *Safe Schools Act* was in force.
[5] These regulations have since been replaced by O. Reg. 472/07 which kept the previous mitigating factors, and added additional "other factors" for consideration.

2. Mitigating Factors and Progressive Discipline

In conjunction with the removal of so-called mandatory discipline, the EAA expanded the number of mitigating and "other factors" for administrators to consider before imposing discipline.[6] A number of these factors incorporate human rights concepts explicitly into the student discipline regime, stemming from a settlement agreement between the Ontario Human Rights Commission (hereinafter the "OHRC") and the Ministry of Education which resolved a complaint initiated by the OHRC against the Ministry regarding the *Safe Schools Act*.

In addition, administrators are required to apply a progressive discipline approach to student misconduct, rather than the zero-tolerance type of approach that was at least perceived to exist under the Safe Schools Regime. One of the "other factors" now required to be taken into account is "whether a progressive discipline approach has been used with the pupil." School boards are also now required to develop policies regarding progressive discipline and these policies must satisfy the requirements set out in the Ministry of Education Policy/Program Memorandum No. 145, released in October 2007 (see Appendix E for PPM 145).[7]

The mitigating factors and progressive discipline are discussed in more detail below under Heading C., "THE APPLICATION OF MITIGATING FACTORS AND PROGRESSIVE DISCIPLINE".

3. Bullying and Off-School Property Conduct

The EAA includes bullying as an activity for which a suspension may be imposed. In addition, the EAA explicitly gives an administrator the power to discipline for an activity occurring off-school property if the activity will impact on the school climate. Therefore, it is now entirely clear that students may be disciplined for what is often called "cyber-bullying", although, arguably this power is not new. See below under Heading D.3., "Addition of Bullying" and D.4., "Off-School Property Conduct" for more detailed discussions about these issues.

---

[6] These factors are set out in O. Reg. 472/07, which was passed in August of 2007 to replace O. Reg. 37/01 and 106/01.

[7] All of the Minister's Policy/Program Memoranda may be obtained on the Ministry of Education website at <http://www.edu.gov.on.ca>.

4. No more Teacher Suspensions

As was expected, the EAA removed the power of teachers to suspend pupils that existed under the Safe Schools Regime. Effectively teachers were not utilizing this power in any event, pursuant to instructions from their federations. Therefore, this amendment to the law now reflects the reality that only principals have been suspending pupils.

5. No More Principal Expulsions

The *Safe Schools Act* empowered principals to expel pupils from their own school for up to one year through a limited expulsion. The EAA removes this power from principals and limits the power to expel solely to school boards, following an expulsion hearing being conducted by at least three trustees. In addition, as explained below, effective February 2008, principals will no longer have the power to deny access to pupils. These changes restrict a principal's power to independently deal with serious safety concerns within his or her own school (*i.e.*, without the further involvement of board trustees). The impact of this change on the ability of principals to maintain a safe school environment remains to be seen.

School boards can now expel a pupil either from the pupil's own school (a "School Expulsion") or from all board schools (a "Board Expulsion").[8] The School Expulsion is comparable to the former limited expulsion, except that the pupil is transferred to a different school by the expulsion committee at the conclusion of the expulsion hearing. The Board Expulsion is similar to the former full expulsion, except that the pupil is only prohibited from attending the schools within his or her own school board rather than all public schools across Ontario, as in the case of a full expulsion. See below under the Heading E., "Expulsions" for a detailed discussion about expulsion procedures.

---

[8] The terms "School Expulsion" and "Board Expulsion" are not used in the legislation, but are utilized in the text for the sake of convenience and clarity.

6. Revisions to Time Periods and Composition of Discipline Committees

The EAA provides that a parent/student has 10 school days within which to appeal a suspension, whereas this was previously determined by school board policy.[9] Unless otherwise agreed, a suspension appeal must now be heard and determined within 15 school days[10] and it must be heard by a committee of at least three trustees.[11] An expulsion hearing must be conducted within 20 school days (unless otherwise agreed)[12] and must now be heard and determined by a committee of at least three trustees.[13] Discipline procedures are discussed in more detail under Heading D, "Suspensions" and E, "Expulsions".

7. Education for Suspended and Expelled Pupils

The EAA requires school boards to provide at least one program for suspended pupils and at least one for expelled pupils. In August of 2007, the Ministry of Education released Policy/Program Memorandum 141 and 142 which set out requirements for the provision of education programs for disciplined pupils (see Appendices B and C for PPM 141 and 142). See below under Heading F, "Education of Suspended and Expelled Pupils" for more details in this regard.

8. Code of Conduct

The *Provincial Code of Conduct*, originally released in April 2000, was revised in October 2007 to reflect the changes to the *Education Act*. The revised *Provincial Code of Conduct* is found in Ministry of Education Policy/Program Memorandum No. 128 (hereinafter "PPM 128" in Appendix A). The PPM provides direction to school boards to review and revise their codes of conduct to make them consistent with the new *Provincial Code of Conduct* by February 1, 2008. If applicable, school boards must also require principals to review and revise their local school codes of conduct by the same deadline. The codes will set out clear

---

[9] In the case of a suspension leading to possible expulsion, the parent, student, or guardian must commence the appeal within five school days of receiving notice of the suspension (rather than 10 school days). See *Education Act*, s. 311.2(1).

[10] *Education Act*, s. 309(6).

[11] *Ibid.*, s. 309(12).

[12] *Ibid.*, s. 311.3(8). This was also a requirement under the Safe Schools Regime.

[13] *Ibid.*, s. 311.3(9). This requirement was added by the EAA.

standards of behaviour expected of all individuals involved in the school system and should be communicated to the school community as required by school board policy. Administrators should keep a record of how and when the *Code of Conduct* was communicated to the students and school community for possible future use in proceedings (*i.e.*, this can be used as evidence to dispute a pupil's position that he or she was not aware that certain conduct was unacceptable).

C. THE APPLICATION OF MITIGATING FACTORS AND PROGRESSIVE DISCIPLINE

1. Mitigating and Other Factors

(a) Overview

The EAA has expanded the number of factors to be considered by administrators before disciplining pupils. As explained above, O. Reg. 472/07 sets out the mitigating factors and "other factors" to be considered at various stages in the discipline process (and in particular, when applying subsections 306(2), 306(4), 310(3), 311.1(4) and clauses 311.3(7)(b) and 311.4(2)(b) of the *Education Act*).[14] Firstly, the regulation specifies that the following mitigating factors "shall be taken into account":

1. The pupil does not have the ability to control his or her behaviour.
2. The pupil does not have the ability to understand the foreseeable consequences of his or her behaviour.
3. The pupil's continuing presence in the school does not create an unacceptable risk to the safety of any person.[15]

These mitigating factors existed under the Safe Schools Regime in Regulations 37/01 and 106/01.[16] The first two factors are particularly relevant in respect of students with special needs, whereas the third factor is a broad factor that could apply in any circumstances.

---

[14] All statutory sections sited to in this text refer to the sections of the *Education Act* as amended by the EAA unless otherwise specified.

[15] O. Reg. 472/07, s. 2. Notably, these factors are identical to those in former O. Reg. 37/01 regarding expulsions and substantially similar to the factors in former O. Reg. 107/01, the only difference being that the last factor in O. Reg. 107/01 referred to an "unacceptable risk to the safety or well-being of any person."

[16] Now replaced by O. Reg. 472/07.

Secondly, the regulation adds the following "other factors" to be taken into account "if they would mitigate the seriousness of the activity" for which the pupil may be or is being disciplined:

1. The pupil's history.
2. Whether a progressive discipline approach has been used with the pupil.
3. Whether the activity for which the pupil may be or is being suspended or expelled was related to any harassment of the pupil because of his or her race, ethnic origin, religion, disability, gender or sexual orientation or to any other harassment.
4. How the suspension or expulsion would affect the pupil's ongoing education.
5. The age of the pupil.
6. In the case of a pupil for whom an individual education plan has been developed,
    i. whether the behaviour was a manifestation of a disability identified in the pupil's individual education plan,
    ii. whether appropriate individualized accommodation has been provided, and
    iii. whether the suspension or expulsion is likely to result in an aggravation or worsening of the pupil's behaviour or conduct.[17]

(b) Application of the Factors

The regulation makes a distinction between the "mitigating factors" and "other factors". While the mitigating factors must always be taken into account, the "other factors" are to be taken into account: "if they would mitigate the seriousness of the activity for which the pupil may be or is being suspended or expelled."[18] In order for an administrator to assess whether each of the "other factors" would mitigate the seriousness of the activity, the administrator must take into account each of these factors in any event. Therefore, regardless of this distinction, administrators should always explicitly consider whether any of these factors would apply to mitigate the conduct.

Notably, under the Safe Schools Regime, administrators were required to consider the "pupil's history", "factors as may be prescribed by regulation" and "such other matters as he or she considers appropriate" in the case of so-called mandatory suspensions and expulsions.[19] The EAA does not require consideration of "such other factors as he or she considers appropriate", but adds the specific list of "other factors" above for

---

[17] O. Reg. 472/07, s. 3.
[18] *Ibid.*
[19] *Education Act*, former subsections s. 306(9) and (19).

consideration. That being said, prior to imposing discipline, an administrator may wish to consider any other matters that the administrator believes may be appropriate (even if they are not listed in the "other factors") in addition to the listed factors.

Many of the "other factors" were included in the terms of a settlement agreement between the Ministry of Education and the OHRC[20] which resolved a human rights complaint initiated against the Ministry by the OHRC regarding the *Safe Schools Act*. Therefore, it is not surprising that many of these factors incorporate human rights concepts explicitly into the student discipline process. This change may give rise to an increased number of human rights complaints within the student discipline process when parties disagree on their interpretations of obligations under the Ontario *Human Rights Code*.

(c) Application of the Factors to Pupils with Special Needs

Administrators should exercise significant caution when considering the discipline of pupils with special needs and should carefully consider the three mitigating factors and the "other factors" which may have particular relevance to pupils with special education needs: (such as 3, 5, 6(i), (ii), and (iii)).[21] In addition, administrators are now specifically required to consider whether accommodations have been made under the Ontario *Human Rights Code*. These changes may lead to some understandable apprehension on the part of administrators when making these determinations, and concerns of exposure to human rights complaints.

Unless and until further guidance is provided in this regard, administrators will need to rely on their own good judgment and the resources available to them to best apply these factors to each situation. Administrators should carefully review all relevant school board policies, procedures and protocols for guidance in this regard. Administrators may also wish to consult with their Supervisory Officer, the pupil's teachers and individuals with special education expertise where appropriate. This will enable the administrator to make an educated determination in respect of each of these factors. In the case of a pupil identified with special needs, the principal should carefully review the IEP and discuss each of the applicable factors with the student's teacher or a special education expert.

---

[20] The terms of this settlement agreement can be found on the OHRC website at the following link: <http://www.ohrc.on.ca/>.
[21] O. Reg. 472/07, s. 3.

The consideration of these factors may well be the most daunting of the tasks required of an administrator under the EAA. However, if an administrator carefully considers these factors, seeks appropriate assistance to make informed decisions, and applies good judgment in this regard (carefully documenting the decision-making process), the administrator's decision should be defensible if brought under legal challenge.

See below under Heading I, "Discipline of Pupils with Special Needs" for further discussion in this regard.

2. Progressive Discipline

Although the concept of progressive discipline was not defined in the EAA or related regulations, the Ministry of Education subsequently provided more direction on this issue through Policy/Program Memorandum 145 (hereinafter "PPM 145"), released in October of 2007 (see Appendix E).

Prior to PPM 145, the notion of progressive discipline was only referenced in one of the "other factors" to be considered before imposing discipline (*i.e.*, "Whether a progressive discipline approach has been used with the pupil".)[22] Therefore, before imposing discipline, an administrator is required to consider whether this factor (*i.e.*, whether a progressive discipline approach has been used) would "mitigate the seriousness of the activity". This essentially means that if a progressive discipline approach was not used with the pupil in the past, this may function to mitigate the seriousness of the incident. That is to say, since the pupil was not given the proper supportive and corrective guidance through a progressive discipline approach in the past, the subsequent misconduct should be treated as less serious than it otherwise would be.

In addition, generally speaking, principals and school boards are required to take a progressive discipline approach before imposing any discipline. PPM 145 requires school boards to implement progressive discipline policies that comply with the PPM and to take a progressive discipline approach that incorporates both early intervention strategies and appropriate supports to address inappropriate behaviour. Therefore, in addition to a principal's requirement to consider progressive discipline as one of the "other factors" if it mitigates the seriousness of the conduct, a principal has a general obligation to take a progressive discipline approach to imposing discipline.

---

[22] O. Reg. 472/07, s. 3.

(a) Definition of Progressive Discipline

PPM 145 describes "progressive discipline" as follows:

> Progressive discipline is a whole-school approach that utilizes a continuum of interventions, supports, and consequences to address inappropriate student behaviour and to build upon strategies that promote positive behaviours described above. When inappropriate behaviour occurs, disciplinary measures should be applied within a framework that shifts the focus from one that is solely punitive to one that is both corrective and supportive. Schools should utilize a range of interventions, supports, and consequences that include learning opportunities for reinforcing positive behaviour while helping students make good choices.
>
> In some circumstances, short-term suspension may be a useful tool. In the case of a serious incident, long-term suspension or expulsion, which is further along the continuum of progressive discipline, may be the response that is required.[23]

(b) Progressive Discipline Policies

As explained, PPM 145 requires school boards to incorporate into their progressive discipline policies both early and ongoing intervention strategies, and strategies for addressing inappropriate behaviour when it occurs.

The PPM stipulates that early and ongoing intervention strategies should provide students with "appropriate supports that address inappropriate behaviour and that would result in an improved school climate."[24] Early interventions may include "contact with parents, detentions, verbal reminders, review of expectations, or a written work assignment with a learning component" and ongoing interventions may include: "meetings with parents, volunteer service to the school community, conflict mediation, peer mentoring, and/or a referral to counselling."[25]

The PPM provides that a school board's strategies for addressing inappropriate behaviour should involve the use of a "range of interventions, supports, and consequences that are developmentally appropriate, and should incorporate opportunities for students to focus on improving behaviour."[26] The PPM also stipulates that consequences for inappropriate behaviour may include "a meeting with parent(s), student

---

[23] Policy/Program Memorandum No. 145 of the Minister of Education regarding "Progressive Discipline and Promoting Positive Student Behavior" (PPM No. 145 in Appendix E).
[24] Ibid.
[25] Ibid.
[26] Ibid.

and principal, referral to a community agency for anger management or substance abuse, and detentions or loss of privilege".[27] PPM 145 also stipulates that "schools are expected to actively engage parents in the progressive discipline approach".[28]

PPM 145 also identifies three factors that should be taken into consideration when determining the most appropriate response to inappropriate behaviour:

- the particular student and circumstances (*e.g.*, mitigating or other factors);
- the nature and severity of the behaviour; and
- the impact on the school climate (*i.e.*, the relationships within the school community).[29]

Therefore, the key elements to consider when administering a progressive discipline approach are: 1) the student's circumstances, 2) the seriousness of the conduct, and 3) the impact of the conduct on the school community. This provides a helpful framework for administrators when considering a response to inappropriate behaviour and should be incorporated into school board policies on progressive discipline.

The PPM requires school boards to satisfy various requirements when developing their policies. For example, board policies must include the following statements:

- The goal of the policy is to support a safe learning and teaching environment in which every student can reach his or her full potential.
- Appropriate action must consistently be taken to address behaviours that are contrary to provincial and board codes of conduct.
- Progressive discipline is an approach that makes use of a continuum of interventions, supports, and consequences, building upon strategies that promote positive behaviours.
- The range of interventions, supports, and consequences used by the board and all schools must be clear and developmentally appropriate, and must include learning opportunities for students in order to reinforce positive behaviours and help students make good choices.
- For students with special education needs, interventions, supports, and consequences must be consistent with the expectations in the student's IEP.

---

[27] *Ibid.*
[28] *Ibid.*
[29] *Ibid.*

- The board, and school administrators, must consider all mitigating and other factors, as required by the Education Act and as set out in Ontario Regulation 472/07.

The policies are expected to be developed through partnerships within the school community and there should be protocols between boards and community agencies to facilitate the delivery of the prevention and intervention programs. Boards are also required to incorporate initial and ongoing staff training on these policies and the policies must be actively communicated to the school community. The PPM also requires boards to establish a monitoring and review process for the board policies[30] and to conduct a cyclical review of their policies and procedures in a timely manner.

Given the flexible approach that is taken in PPM 145, each school board's progressive discipline policy will vary depending on the school board's particular needs and available resources. Principals should carefully review all applicable policies, procedures and protocols to determine the school board practices and available resources and the steps that the principal is required to take in this regard.

(c) Progressive Discipline involving Students with Special Needs

PPM 145 specifically requires that interventions, supports and consequences for pupils with special education needs must be "consistent with the student's strengths, needs, goals, and expectations contained in his or her Individual Education Plan (IEP)."[31] Essentially administrators are required to accommodate pupils in a manner that is consistent with their specific needs when imposing discipline. This obligation to accommodate students' disabilities has always existed under the Ontario *Human Rights Code*; however, the *Education Act* specifically requires the accommodations to be consistent with the student's "strength's, needs, goals and expectations" set out in her Individual Education Plan (hereinafter "IEP"). Principals should, therefore, take care to consider each of these elements of the pupil's IEP to tailor the progressive discipline approach to each of these aspects.

---

[30] The PPM states that this process should include performance indicators that should be developed in consultation with teachers, students, parents, school councils, their Special Education Advisory Committee, their Parent Involvement Committee and community services providers.

[31] Policy/Program Memorandum No. 145 of the Minister of Education regarding "Progressive Discipline and Promoting Positive Student Behavior" (PPM No. 145 in Appendix E).

Of course, in addition, as explained above, administrators must carefully consider the mitigating and other factors before imposing discipline in respect of special needs pupils. See also below under Heading I, "Discipline of Pupils with Special Needs".

D. SUSPENSIONS

1. Overview

Suspensions are addressed in sections 306 to 309 of the *Education Act* and in Ontario Regulation 472/07 (hereinafter "O. Reg. 472/07").[32] When considering whether to impose a suspension, a principal should review this legislation as well as all relevant school board policies, procedures or guidelines regarding suspensions. Further, the principal should become familiar with the forms required when suspending a pupil.

Section 306 requires that a principal consider whether to suspend a pupil if the principal believes:

> that the pupil has engaged in any of the following activities while at school, at a school-related activity or in other circumstances where engaging in the activity will have an impact on the school climate:
>
> 1. Uttering a threat to inflict serious bodily harm on another person.
> 2. Possessing alcohol or illegal drugs.
> 3. Being under the influence of alcohol.
> 4. Swearing at a teacher or at another person in a position of authority.
> 5. Committing an act of vandalism that causes extensive damage to school property at the pupil's school or to property located on the premises of the pupil's school.
> 6. Bullying.
> 7. Any other activity that is an activity for which a principal may suspend a pupil under a policy of the board.[33]

Therefore, if a principal believes that the pupil has engaged in any of the activities listed above or those listed in school board policy pursuant to "7", the principal must consider whether to suspend the pupil.

---

[32] This regulation replaced O. Reg. 106/01 (suspension of a pupil) and O. Reg. 37/01 (expulsion of a pupil).
[33] *Education Act*, s. 306.

2. Interpretation of Listed Activities

Under the Safe Schools Regime, principals sometimes faced challenges determining whether a pupil committed the listed infractions which gave rise to so-called mandatory discipline. Some principals were under a mistaken belief that since the listed infractions resembled criminal offences the principal had to be satisfied beyond a reasonable doubt that the legal elements of a criminal offence took place before concluding that the pupil "commit the infraction". In fact, when considering whether a pupil has engaged in certain conduct, the principal is only required to be satisfied on a balance of probabilities (*i.e.*, that it is more likely than not) that the conduct took place. Given that the EAA has removed the term "infraction" and eliminated the language of mandatory discipline, it is hoped that there will not be continued confusion in this regard.

Administrators should look to school board policies and procedures to review their school board's definitions regarding each of the listed "activities". In addition, administrators will be required to use their best judgment in order to fairly determine whether they believe the student engaged in the activity.

3. Addition of "Bullying"

All of the activities listed in section 306 (with the exception of bullying) were previously considered "infractions" for which suspensions were "mandatory" under former subsection 306(1) of the Safe Schools Regime. The EAA added bullying as an activity for which suspension may now be imposed.

In October of 2007, the Ministry of Education released Policy/Program Memorandum No. 144 entitled: "Bullying Prevention and Intervention" (hereinafter "PPM 144" in Appendix D) which provides direction to school boards regarding this issue.

(a) Definition of Bullying

PPM 144 provides the following definition of bullying:

> Bullying is typically a form of repeated, persistent, and aggressive behaviour directed at an individual or individuals that is intended to cause (or should be known to cause) fear and distress and/or harm to another person's body, feelings, self-

esteem, or reputation. Bullying occurs in a context where there is a real or perceived power imbalance.[34]

When considering whether a student has engaged in "bullying" under section 306 of the *Act*, an administrator should review the conduct in light of this definition. The definition is fairly broad and a principal should look to school board policies and procedures and/or consult with his or her Supervisory Officer for further guidance in this regard. If the principal concludes that the activity constitutes bullying, the principal must also consider the mitigating and other factors and apply the progressive discipline approach set out by school board policy when considering possible discipline. In addition, the administrator will be required to apply the school board policies regarding bullying prevention and intervention as they apply to particular incidents of student misconduct, as discussed below.

In addition to defining "bullying", the PPM provides specific examples of power imbalances (which may be real or perceived) and gives concrete examples of bullying as follows:

> Students may attain or maintain power over others in the school through real or perceived differences. Some areas of difference may be size, strength, age, intelligence, economic status, social status, solidarity of peer group, religion, ethnicity, disability, need for special education, sexual orientation, family circumstances, gender and race.
>
> Bullying is a dynamic of unhealthy interaction that can take many forms. It can be physical (e.g., hitting, pushing, tripping), verbal (*e.g.*, name calling, mocking, or making sexist, racist, or homophobic comments), or social (*e.g.*, excluding others from a group, spreading gossip or rumours). It may also occur through the use of technology (*e.g.*, spreading rumours, images, or hurtful comments through the use of e-mail, cellphones, text messaging, Internet websites, or other technology).[35]

Although these further examples are not incorporated into the "bullying" definition itself, they provide further guidance as to how the Ministry of Education interprets the term "bullying". Since these examples cover a broad range of conduct, it is expected that administrators will face pressure from parents of students that they believe to be victims of bullying pursuant to this PPM in a broad range of circumstances. Administrators should assess each situation on a case-by-case basis in order to determine whether the administrator believes that the conduct should be considered "bullying" under the definition set out above, and whether it warrants discipline in the circumstances, or some other form of appropriate

---

[34] Policy/Program Memorandum No. 144 of the Minister of Education regarding "Bullying Prevention and Intervention" (PPM No. 144 in Appendix D).
[35] *Ibid.*

intervention. In all cases, the administrator should keep detailed documentation of his or her decision in case it is challenged.

(b) Positive School Climate

PPM 144 explains that it is crucial for boards to maintain a positive school climate for the prevention of bullying, explaining that when "relationships are founded in mutual acceptance and inclusion, and modelled by all, a culture of respect becomes the norm."[36] The PPM states that to help achieve a positive school environment, boards and schools should actively promote and support positive behaviours that reflect their character development initiatives. The following examples of characteristics of a positive school climate are provided in the PPM:

- Students and staff feel safe and are safe.
- Healthy and inclusive relationships are promoted.
- Students are encouraged to be positive leaders in their school community.
- All partners are actively engaged.
- Bullying prevention messages are reinforced through programs addressing discrimination based on such factors as age, race, sexual orientation, gender, faith, disability, ethnicity, and socio-economic disadvantage.
- Improvement of learning outcomes for all students is emphasized.[37]

(c) School Board Policies on Bullying

PPM 144 requires school boards and schools to develop and implement policies on bullying prevention and intervention consistent with the PPM by February 1, 2008, or to review and revise their existing bullying policies to ensure their consistency with the PPM.[38] The policies must provide for training (initial and ongoing) for board personnel at the school

---

[36] PPM 144 includes this quote from the *Safe Schools Policy and Practice: An Agenda for Action*, Report of the Safe Schools Action Team (Toronto: June 2006), at 8.

[37] Policy/Program Memorandum No. 144 of the Minister of Education regarding "Bullying Prevention and Intervention" (PPM No. 144 in Appendix D).

[38] When developing their policies, school boards are required to consult with a number of groups, including school councils, parents, principals, teachers, students, Parent Involvement Committee, Special Education Advisory Committee, community partners, social service agencies, members of Aboriginal communities (*e.g.*, Elders) and "those groups that are traditionally not consulted". *(Notably, such groups are not specifically identified in the PPM.)*

board and school levels. The PPM requires that the policies provide for a review and monitoring process[39] and requires boards to actively communicate their policies and the definition of bullying to the school community.[40]

PPM 144 also requires that each school have a safe schools team responsible for school safety which is composed of at least one student (where appropriate), one parent, one teacher, one support staff member, one community partner, and the principal, with one staff chair. The PPM specifies that an existing school committee can assume this role. The specific mandate of the safe schools team is unclear, as the PPM simply states that it will be "responsible for school safety." This may lead to some confusion without further direction from the Ministry of Education.

PPM 144 requires boards to include a number of components into their bullying policies. For example, the policies must include the following statements:

- Bullying adversely affects students' ability to learn.
- Bullying adversely affects healthy relationships and the school climate.
- Bullying adversely affects a school's ability to educate its students.
- Bullying will not be accepted on school property, at school-related activities, on school buses, or in any other circumstances (*e.g.*, online) where engaging in bullying will have a negative impact on the school climate.[41]

The policies are required to include comprehensive strategies for prevention and for intervention to address incidents of bullying.

The comprehensive prevention strategy must include expectations for appropriate student behaviour, teaching strategies that focus on developing healthy relationships, student participation in bullying prevention training, and leadership initiatives.

The comprehensive strategy to address bullying incidents must provide for appropriate and timely interventions consistent with a progressive discipline approach. Strategies will range from early interventions to more

---

[39] The PPM indicates that this process should include: "an analysis of the school climate through anonymous surveys of the students, staff members, and parents done on a regular cycle, as determined by the board" and "performance indicators for monitoring, reviewing and evaluating the effectiveness of the board's bullying prevention and intervention policies."

[40] The PPM indicates that boards "should make every effort to share this information with parents whose first language is a language other than English or French."

[41] Policy/Program Memorandum No. 144 of the Minister of Education regarding "Bullying Prevention and Intervention" (PPM No. 144 in Appendix D).

intensive interventions in the case of persistent bullying, with possible referral to community or social services agencies. Board policies must provide for ongoing interventions to sustain and promote positive student behaviour. They must also include procedures for the safe reporting of bullying incidents to minimize the possibility of reprisal and provide support for victims and all persons involved in bullying incidents. In addition, the policies must include teaching strategies and training for staff and others in contact with students. The policies must clearly set out the roles and responsibilities of all members of the school community and must be actively communicated to the school community.

4. Off-School Property Conduct

The EAA explicitly gives a principal the power to discipline for off-school property conduct if "engaging in the activity will have an impact on the school climate".[42] Conduct occurring at school or while engaged in a "school-related activity" has always been subject to discipline. Arguably, "school related activity" was intended to be broadly interpreted, and in many cases it has been. The legislative change solidifies the fact that off-school conduct may properly lead to discipline when it will impact the school. However, the term "will impact on the school climate" is not defined in the EAA or in other Ministry of Education materials. As a result, it is expected that conflicts will continue to arise when administrators discipline pupils for off-school property conduct.

As indicated above, the combined effect of this change and the addition of bullying as a listed activity is that "cyber-bullying" clearly falls within the scope of the new legislation. While there can be no dispute (at least in principle) that discipline can be imposed in cases of cyber-bullying, it is likely that disputes will occur as to whether the off-school property conduct will impact on the school climate. In the writer's opinion, this definition should be broadly and liberally interpreted (whether in the case of cyber-bullying or otherwise). Principals should be aware that if they do not give this term a broad interpretation, in addition to potential risk to their students and staff, the principal and school board may face liability for failing to maintain a safe school environment.

---

[42] *Education Act*, s. 306(1).

5. Mitigating and Other Factors

When determining whether to suspend, a principal must consider any mitigating or other factors as prescribed in the regulations.[43] See above under Heading C., "The Application of Mitigating Factors and Progressive Discipline" in this regard.

6. Duration

The duration of a suspension is from one day to 20 days and a suspended pupil cannot attend at his or her school or engage in any school-related activities. When determining the length of a suspension under this section, the principal must take into account any mitigating or other factors as prescribed in the regulations.[44] See above under Heading C, "The Application of Mitigating Factors and Progressive Discipline".

Notably, this provision does not include a pupil's removal from school for less than one day which is not considered to be a suspension under the EAA. Therefore, the right to appeal a suspension described below does not apply when a pupil is removed from school (or from class) for less than one day.[45] Before the EAA, suspensions of one day or less were exempt from appeal.[46] The difference now is that one-day suspensions will now be subject to appeal. Suspensions for one-day were a tool often used by administrators as a "time out" for students who are occasionally disruptive. It remains to be seen how this change will impact on the manner by which administrators impose short-term suspensions in the future.

The EAA also specifies that a principal cannot suspend a pupil more than once for the same occurrence.[47] Therefore, once a principal has suspended a pupil for a particular incident, the principal cannot subsequently suspend the pupil again in respect of the identical incident. This provision should not be interpreted to prevent an administrator from suspending a pupil who, after being suspended, engages in identical or similar conduct on a subsequent occasion, which may itself properly give rise to discipline.

---

[43] *Ibid.*, s. 306(2).
[44] *Ibid.*, s. 306(4).
[45] Initially Bill 212 provided for the appeal of suspensions of any duration, including the removal from one class. This change was incorporated after consultation with stakeholders before the Standing Committee on General Government.
[46] *Education Act*, s. 308(4) under the Safe Schools Regime.
[47] *Education Act*, s. 307.

7. Completion of Forms

When suspending a pupil, a principal must complete the forms required by school board policy/procedures or by the Ministry of Education such as the Suspension Form, and a Violent Incident Form (if applicable).[48] When completing these forms, principals should take care to ensure that the information recorded is accurate, objective, and includes only facts that are supported by the evidence.

8. Notice of Suspension

A principal who suspends under this section must: (i) inform the pupil's teacher of the suspension; and, (ii) make all reasonable efforts to inform the pupil's parent or guardian of the suspension within 24 hours of imposing the suspension, unless the pupil is over 18 years old or is 16 or 17 years old and has withdrawn from parental control.[49]

The principal is also required to ensure that written notice is given promptly to the following persons: (i) the pupil; (ii) the pupil's parent or guardian unless the pupil is over 18 years old or is 16 or 17 years old and has withdrawn from parental control; and (iii) other persons as specified by board policy.[50] The written notice must include the following:

1. The reason for the suspension.
2. The duration of the suspension.
3. Information about any program for suspended pupils to which the pupil is assigned.
4. Information about the right to appeal the suspension under section 309, including,
    i. a copy of the board policies and guidelines governing the appeal established by the board under subsection 302 (6), and
    ii. the name and contact information of the supervisory officer to whom notice of the appeal must be given under subsection 309 (2).[51]

---

[48] See the Ministry of Education Violence Free School Policy, 1994.
[49] *Education Act*, s. 308(1).
[50] *Ibid.*, s. 308(2).
[51] *Ibid.*, s. 308(3).

9. Suspension Appeal Process

(a) Who may Appeal?

A principal's decision to suspend may be appealed by the following persons: (i) parent or guardian (unless the pupil is 18 years old or 16 or 17 years old and has withdrawn from parental control), (ii) a pupil who is 18 years old, or who is 16 or 17 and has withdrawn from parental control, or (iii) other persons as specified by board policy.[52]

(b) Notice of Appeal

The person appealing must give written notice of the intention to appeal to the supervisory officer designated to receive notices of intentions to appeal within 10 school days of the commencement of the suspension.[53] Once the Notice of Appeal has been received, the board must promptly contact every person entitled to appeal the suspension to inform them of the notice of intention to appeal.[54]

(c) Optional Suspension Review Process

The person appealing the suspension may contact the designated supervisory officer (who has the powers and duties set out in board policy) to discuss any matter respecting the appeal of the suspension.[55] This step provides an option similar to the suspension review process in the Safe Schools Regime; however, it is at the option of the parent/student, rather than being mandatory.

(d) Suspension Appeal Hearing Process

The board (by a committee of at least three trustees)[56] is required to hear and determine the appeal within 15 school days of receipt of notice of the intention to appeal, unless otherwise agreed,[57] and the board cannot refuse to deal with the appeal as a result of a deficiency in the notice of appeal.[58]

---

[52] *Ibid.*, s. 309.
[53] *Ibid.*, ss. 309(2), (3).
[54] *Ibid.*, s. 309(4).
[55] *Ibid.*, s. 309(5).
[56] *Ibid.*, s. 309(12).
[57] *Ibid.*, s. 309(6). Initially Bill 212 required the matters to be heard within 10 school days; however, this was extended to 15 following submissions before the Standing Committee on General Government.
[58] *Ibid.*, s. 309(6).

These new procedural requirements may lead to scheduling difficulties for certain school boards, which may have difficulty finding three trustees to hear a suspension appeal within 15 school days. If compliance with the 15 school day appeal period becomes systemically impossible, then arguably a school board unable to meet the time-line (despite reasonable efforts) would have no jurisdiction to overturn a suspension outside the time-line without the consent of the parties, and arguably the suspension would stand. In these circumstances, an aggrieved student may seek to pursue the matter through the courts.

A suspension appeal is conducted as required by board policy. These procedures vary across school boards. Some school boards have taken the position that suspension appeals can be processed in writing (without an oral hearing), while others conduct more formal oral hearings pursuant to the *Statutory Powers Procedure Act*. Given that the *Education Act* now requires that suspension appeals be heard and determined by a committee of at least three trustees, it is expected that most boards will conduct suspension appeals through the more formal process of an oral hearing, failing which, they may be subject to legal challenge.

(e) Parties to Suspension Appeal

The parties to the appeal are the following:
(1) The principal who suspended the pupil;
(2) The pupil, if the pupil is at least 18 years old, or 16 or 17 years old and has withdrawn from parental control;
(3) The pupil's parent or guardian, if the pupil's parent or guardian appealed the decision to suspend the pupil;
(4) The person who appealed the decision to suspend the pupil, if the decision was appealed by a person other than the pupil or the pupil's parent or guardian; and
(5) Such other persons as may be specified by board policy.

(f) Pupil's Right to Attend

The EAA provides that a pupil who is not a party to the appeal has the right to be present at the appeal and to make a statement on his or her own behalf.[59] These provisions clarify the role of a pupil who is not a party in the appeal process, *i.e.*, the pupil is entitled to attend at the appeal and to make a statement on his or her own behalf.

---

[59] *Ibid.*, s. 309(9).

(g) Powers of Board Committee

On appeal, the board committee must: (i) confirm the suspension and duration; (ii) confirm the suspension but shorten its duration and order that the record be amended accordingly; or (iii) quash the suspension and order that the record of the suspension be expunged.[60] This decision is final.[61]

As explained above, the school board can authorize a committee of at least three members of the board to exercise and perform powers and duties on behalf of the board, and may impose conditions and restrictions on the committee.[62] Previously there was no minimum requirement for the number of trustees to hear suspension appeals, and they were sometimes conducted by a single trustee.

E. EXPULSIONS

1. Overview

Expulsions are addressed in sections 310 and 311 of the *Education Act* and in Ontario Regulation 472/07.[63] When a principal considers recommending an expulsion, a principal should review this legislation as well as all relevant school board policies and procedures and Ministry of Education documentation regarding expulsions. Further, the principal should be familiar with the forms that he or she is required to complete in this process.

Subsection 310(1) sets out a number of activities for which a pupil must be suspended and which may lead to possible expulsion. A principal is required to suspend a pupil and must conduct an investigation if he or she believes that the pupil has engaged in any of the following activities "while at school, at a school-related activity or in other circumstances where engaging in the activity will have an impact on the school climate":

(1) Possessing a weapon, including possessing a firearm;
(2) Using a weapon to cause or to threaten bodily harm to another person;
(3) Committing physical assault on another person that causes bodily harm requiring treatment by a medical practitioner;
(4) Committing sexual assault;

---

[60] *Ibid.*, s. 309(10).
[61] *Ibid.*, s. 309(11).
[62] *Ibid.*, s. 309(12).
[63] As indicated, O. Reg. 472/07 replaced O. Reg. 37/01 (Expulsion of a Pupil) and O. Reg. 106/01 (Suspension of a Pupil).

(5) Trafficking in weapons or in illegal drugs;
(6) Committing robbery;
(7) Giving alcohol to a minor; or,
(8) Any other activity that, under a policy of a board, is an activity for which a principal must suspend a pupil and, therefore in accordance with this Part, conduct an investigation to determine whether to recommend to the board that the pupil be expelled.[64]

These listed activities are the same infractions which, under former subsection 309(1) of the Safe Schools Regime, gave rise to so-called mandatory expulsions.

The real issue is to identify the threshold required for a principal to reach a belief that the pupil has engaged in one of these activities which then triggers the suspension of the pupil. Further, as noted below, the principal must take into account mitigating or other factors when determining the duration of the suspension. An administrator must conduct enough of a preliminary investigation to come to the belief that the pupil has engaged in any of these activities and to consider the mitigating or other factors to decide the appropriate duration of the suspension.

Principals should review relevant school board policies for guidance regarding the steps that they are expected to take before imposing the initial suspension, as they will vary across school boards.

2. Duration of Suspension Pending Possible Expulsion

The initial suspension can be of a duration of up to 20 school days and when considering its duration, the principal is required to take into account "any mitigating or other factors prescribed by the regulations."[65] See above under Heading C, "The Application of Mitigating Factors and Progressive Discipline". The requirement to consider mitigating factors in respect of the duration of the suspension may raise practical difficulties. For example, a principal may impose a 10 school day suspension (based on mitigating factors), but it may not be possible to schedule the expulsion hearing for 15 school days. The issue would arise as to whether the pupil should be entitled to return to school even though the expulsion hearing has not yet been held.[66] The EAA does not deal with what happens in these circumstances. In any event, if a principal imposes a suspension of under 20 days, efforts should be made to schedule the expulsion hearing before

---

[64] *Education Act*, s. 310(1).
[65] *Ibid.*, s. 310(3).
[66] *Ibid.*, s. 310(3).

the suspension is served. If this is not possible and if the parents/pupil are not prepared to keep the pupil out of school pending the expulsion hearing, the administrator and/or school board will be required to decide whether the pupil should be permitted to return to school in the interim. School boards and/or principals should consult with legal counsel to ensure that the proper steps are taken in this regard.

3. Education for Pupils Suspended Pending Possible Expulsion

The principal must assign a pupil suspended under this section to a program for suspended pupils as required by any policies or guidelines issued by the Minister.[67] See below under Heading F, "Education of Suspended and Expelled Pupils".

4. Notice of Suspension

A principal who suspends a pupil under this section must: (i) notify the pupil's teacher of the suspension; and (ii) make all reasonable efforts to inform the pupil's parent or guardian of the suspension within 24 hours of the suspension being imposed, unless the pupil is at least 18 years old or 16 or 17 years old and has withdrawn from parental control.[68]

The principal is also required to promptly give written notice to the following: (i) the pupil; (ii) the pupil's parent or guardian, unless the pupil is at least 18 years old or 16 or 17 years old and has withdrawn from parental control; and (iii) other persons as specified by board policy.[69]

The written notice must include the following:
1. The reason for the suspension.
2. The duration of the suspension.
3. Information about any program for suspended pupils to which the pupil is assigned.
4. Information about the investigation the principal will conduct to determine whether to recommend expulsion.
5. A statement indicating that,
   i. there is no immediate right to appeal the suspension,
   ii. if the principal does not recommend to the board that the pupil be expelled, the suspension will become subject to appeal, and

---

[67] *Ibid.*, s. 310(4).
[68] *Ibid.*, s. 311(1).
[69] *Ibid.*, s. 311(2).

iii. if there is an expulsion hearing, the suspension may be addressed by parties at the hearing.[70]

5. Investigation

The principal is required to promptly conduct an investigation to determine whether to recommend that the pupil be expelled.[71] As indicated above, the principal will have already investigated enough to arrive at the belief that the pupil engaged in the activity and to have considered mitigating and other factors to determine the appropriate duration. In any event, a more thorough investigation must now be conducted to determine whether to recommend expulsion of the pupil.

The EAA provides that the investigation must be conducted in accordance with board policy, and the principal has the powers and duties set out in the policy; therefore, a principal should follow the board policies and procedures in this regard. Although the Ministry of Education is empowered to establish policies and guidelines with respect to principals' investigations, to date, none have been released.[72]

The EAA specifically requires that a principal make "all reasonable efforts" to speak with the following individuals: (i) the pupil; (ii) the pupil's parent or guardian unless the pupil is at least 18 years old or is 16 or 17 years old and has withdrawn from parental control; and (iii) any other person whom the principal "has reason to believe may have relevant information." [73]

Therefore, although at this point, the principal will have already conducted a preliminary inquiry into the events in question, the principal is further required to conduct a subsequent investigation including the steps above (if not already taken) to determine whether an expulsion should be recommended.

As indicated above, the difficulty is in determining how much investigation should be done before the initial suspension is imposed and what further investigation remains to be conducted following the suspension in order to decide whether to recommend an expulsion. In any event, it is clear that a principal must ensure the steps set out in the EAA are taken prior to determining whether to expel a pupil.

---

[70] *Ibid.*, s. 311(3).
[71] *Ibid.*, s. 311.1.
[72] *Ibid.*, s. 301(6.1).
[73] *Ibid.*, s. 311.1(3).

6. General Tips for Conducting Investigations

Principals should review relevant school board policies, procedures and protocols in this regard, which will provide guidance to the principal regarding the steps to be followed in investigations.

Principals should also refer to the local Police/School Board Protocol which will provide detailed direction for conducting an investigation.[74] The protocol will also address the legal rights of an accused pupil under the *Youth Criminal Justice Act* and the *Canadian Charter of Rights and Freedoms* and will outline procedures for search and seizure. The protocol will also discuss police involvement in school incidents. Generally speaking it is important for principals to maintain a good working relationship with the police, who will have ongoing contact with the school. As a result, it is important for principals to coordinate with the police when conducting the independent school investigation, to ensure that the principal is not interfering with the police investigation.

The investigation of an incident which may lead to discipline should be done in a thorough manner. As required by the EAA, the principal must make all reasonable efforts to interview the pupil, and parent (if applicable), and other individuals who may have relevant information. Interviews should be conducted as soon as possible after the incident (of course after dealing with any emergency medical issues) to ensure the best recollection possible of the witnesses.

All interviews should be conducted in an objective manner, *i.e.*, the principal should not suggest to the witnesses the answers that he or she is expecting to receive. Questions should be open-ended, to ensure that the witness provides an independent account of what took place. The interviews should be well-documented by detailed notes, which provide an accurate account of the witnesses' information, and are also expressed in an objective manner. Principals should be aware that they may be required to provide these interview notes to the pupil's parent or legal counsel in the course of a discipline proceeding.

A principal is often required to assess the credibility of witnesses in an investigation. If the principal has specific reason for questioning the credibility of a certain witness, this should be noted in the documentation as well. See Appendix F for a summary of *S.J. v. Toronto Catholic District*

---

[74] In July of 2007 the Ministry of Education directed school boards to review these local protocols to ensure consistency with the Provincial Model and indicated that in future, boards will be required to submit these protocols for review to ensure such consistency.

School Board,[75] wherein a principal's decision to impose a limited expulsion on a pupil was upheld by the Ontario Divisional Court upon judicial review.

7. Mitigating or Other Factors

When considering whether to recommend that the pupil be expelled, a principal is required to again take into account any mitigating or other factors prescribed by the regulations.[76] See above under Heading C, "The Application of Mitigating Factors and Progressive Discipline".

8. Steps to Follow Where Expulsion is Not Recommended

(a) Review of Initial Suspension

If the principal does not recommend expulsion, the principal must review the initial suspension and either: (i) confirm the suspension and its duration; (ii) confirm the suspension but shorten its duration and amend the record in this regard; or (iii) withdraw the suspension and expunge the record of the suspension.[77] The legislation does not specify that when reviewing the suspension the principal must again consider the mitigating or other factors. However, given that these factors were required to be considered when the suspension was first imposed, the principal should also consider the mitigating and other factors when reviewing the suspension, otherwise this decision upon the review may be subject to challenge.

(b) Written Notice

After the principal's review of the initial suspension, the principal is required to promptly give to the individuals entitled to notice of the suspension under section 311 (*i.e.*, the pupil, parent, or guardian (if required) and other persons required by board policy),[78] written notice

---

[75] [2006] O.J. No. 2878, 214 O.A.C. 39, 50 Admin. L.R. (4th) 243, 143 C.R.R. (2d) 170, 150 A.C.W.S. (3d) 83 (Ont. S.C.J.); supp. [2006] O.J. No. 3902, 216 O.A.C. 204, 50 Admin. L.R. (4th) 261, 152 A.C.W.S. (3d) 42 (Ont. Div. Ct.).

[76] *Education Act*, s. 311.1(4).

[77] *Ibid.*, s. 311.1(5). The new obligation for a principal to review the initial suspension is arguably unnecessary, essentially codifying a power that principals already possess.

[78] *Ibid.*, ss. 311.1(6) and 311(2).

containing the following information: (i) a statement indicating that the pupil is not subject to an expulsion hearing; (ii) a statement indicating whether the principal has confirmed the suspension, reduced its duration, or withdrawn the suspension; and (iii) if the initial suspension was not withdrawn, information about the right to appeal the suspension including: a copy of the board's suspension appeal policies and guidelines and the contact information for the supervisory officer to whom the notice of appeal must be provided.[79]

(c) Appeal of Initial Suspension

If the suspension is not withdrawn, the suspension may be appealed and section 309 (modified as necessary) applies to the appeal except that: (1) a person entitled to appeal must give written notice within five school days of receiving notice of the suspension;[80] and (2) if the principal shortened the duration of the suspension, the appeal is from the reduced suspension.[81]

9. Steps to Follow where Expulsion is Recommended

(a) Report regarding Recommendation

Following the investigation, if the principal recommends expulsion, he or she must prepare a report that contains the following: (i) a summary of the principal's findings; (ii) whether the principal recommends a School Expulsion or a Board Expulsion; (iii) the principal's recommendation regarding the type of school that may benefit the pupil if the pupil is given a School Expulsion, or, the type of program for expelled pupils that may benefit the pupil if he or she is given a Board Expulsion.

The principal is required to promptly provide the report to the board and to all persons to whom the principal was required to give notice of the suspension.[82]

---

[79] *Ibid.*, s. 311.1(6).
[80] *Ibid.*, s. 300(3) states that notice is deemed to be given five school days after a letter was sent by mail (or otherwise sent), or one school day after the day it was sent by fax or otherwise electronically.
[81] *Ibid.*, s. 311.2.
[82] *Ibid.*, s. 311.1(8).

(b) Written Notice

At the same time that the principal provides the Report, the Principal must provide to all individuals entitled to notice of the suspension, written notice containing the following:

1. A statement that the pupil will be subject to an expulsion hearing;
2. A copy of the school board policies and guidelines regarding expulsion hearings;
3. A statement that the person has the right to respond to the principal's report;
4. Detailed information regarding the procedures and possible outcomes of the expulsion hearing, including information explaining that:
    i. if the board does not expel the pupil, the initial suspension will be confirmed, shortened or withdrawn;
    ii. the parties are entitled to make submissions regarding whether the initial suspension should be confirmed, shortened or withdrawn;
    iii. a board's decision regarding the initial suspension is final and not subject to appeal;
    iv. if the board imposes a School Expulsion, the board will assign the pupil to another board school; and,
    v. if the board imposes a Board Expulsion, the board will assign the pupil to a program for expelled pupils.
5. The name and contact information of the supervisory officer whom the person may contact to discuss any matter respecting the expulsion hearing.[83]

As indicated, this latter provision may serve as a means of informal resolution of expulsion matters prior to proceeding to a expulsion hearing. By inviting the parent/pupil to pursue informal discussions concerning any matter regarding the expulsion hearing, it may open communications to facilitate early resolution of such matters.

(c) Response to Report

A person entitled to receive the principal's report can respond in writing to the principal and the board[84] and this response will be considered by the board committee at the expulsion hearing.[85]

---

[83] *Ibid.*, s. 311.1(9). This refers to the informal suspension review process discussed above under Heading D.9.(c), "Optional Suspension Review Process".

(d) Expulsion Hearing

Where a principal recommends an expulsion, the board is required to hold an expulsion hearing. The board has the powers and duties specified by board policy and the hearing must be conducted as required by board policy.[86] Principals should review the applicable board policies and procedures regarding expulsion hearings which will specify the steps to be followed at the hearing.

(e) Board Committee Requirements

The board may authorize a committee of at least three trustees to exercise its powers and duties.[87] Prior to the EAA, there was no minimum requirement specified for the number of trustees on the committee in the *Education Act*, nor is there a minimum requirement found in the *Statutory Powers Procedure Act*,[88] which applies to expulsion hearings.

The board committee must hear and determine the expulsion within 20 school days, unless the parties agree otherwise, as was required under the Safe Schools Regime.[89] The scheduling of expulsion hearings before three trustees within this time period will likely become even more challenging for some boards in light of the new procedural requirements that suspension appeals must be heard and determined within 15 school days before three trustees.

(f) Parties to an Expulsion Hearing

The parties to an expulsion hearing are: (i) the principal; (ii) the pupil if the pupil is at least 18 years old or 16 or 17 years old and has withdrawn from parental control; (iii) the pupil's parent or guardian, unless, the pupil is 18 years old or 16 or 17 and has withdrawn from parental control; and (iv) such other persons as may be specified by board policy.[90]

The EAA also provides that a pupil who is not a party has the right to be present at the hearing and to make a statement on his or her own behalf.[91] This provisions clarifies the role that such a pupil will play in the proceedings.

---

[84] *Ibid.*, s. 311.1(10).
[85] *Ibid.*, s. 311.2(7)(c).
[86] *Ibid.*, s. 311.3.
[87] *Ibid.*, s. 311.3(9).
[88] R.S.O. 1990, c. S.22.
[89] *Education Act*, s. 311.3(8).
[90] *Ibid.*, s. 311.3(3).
[91] *Ibid.*, s. 311.3(4).

(g) Submissions at Expulsion Hearing

During the expulsion hearing, the board committee is required to: (i) consider the submissions of each party in whatever form; (ii) solicit the views of all parties regarding whether, if expelled, a School Expulsion or Board Expulsion should be imposed; and (iii) solicit the views of all parties regarding whether if the pupil is not expelled, the board should confirm the initial suspension of the pupil, reduce its duration, or withdraw the suspension.[92]

(h) Decision of Board Committee

After the hearing, the board committee will decide whether the pupil should be expelled and if so, whether to impose a School Expulsion or a Board Expulsion.[93]

When making these decisions the board must consider all submissions and views of the parties, any mitigating or other factors prescribed by regulation, and any written response to the principal's report.[94] Of course, the board committee should consider all relevant evidence adduced at the hearing, including the principal's report itself, although this is not specifically listed in this provision. Also see above under Heading C, "Application of Mitigating Factors and Progressive Discipline" regarding the board committee's consideration of mitigating and other factors and progressive discipline in the hearing.

10. Steps to Follow where Pupil is not Expelled

(a) Board Committee to Hear Appeal of Initial Suspension

If the board committee does not expel the pupil, the board will: (i) confirm the initial suspension; (ii) confirm the suspension but shorten its duration and order that the record be amended; or (iii) quash the suspension and order that the record of the suspension be expunged.[95]

When making this determination, the board must consider any submissions of the parties and any mitigating or other factors prescribed by

---

[92] *Ibid.*, s. 311.3(5).
[93] *Ibid.*, s. 311.3(6).
[94] *Ibid.*, s. 311.3(7).
[95] *Ibid.*, s. 311.4(1).

regulation.[96] See above under Heading C, "Application of Mitigating Factors and Progressive Discipline". The board's decision is final.[97]

(b) Written Notice of Board Committee Decisions

The board committee is required to give written notice to all parties to the hearing that contains the following information: (i) a statement that the pupil is not expelled; and (ii) a statement indicating whether the board committee confirmed the initial suspension, reduced the duration, or has withdrawn the suspension.[98]

11. Steps to Follow where Pupil is Expelled

(a) Assignment of Expelled Pupil

The board must assign a pupil who has been expelled to:

(i) another school within the board, where it imposes a School Expulsion; or

(ii) a program for expelled students, where it imposes a Board Expulsion.[99]

See below under Heading F, "Education of Suspended and Expelled Pupils" for information regarding the requirements of programs for expelled students.

(b) Written Notice of Board Committee Decisions

The board must ensure that written notice of the expulsion is given promptly to: (i) all parties to the hearing; and (ii) the pupil, if he or she was not a party to the hearing.[100]

This written notice must include:

(i) the reason for the expulsion;

(ii) a statement indicating whether the pupil is expelled from the pupil's own school or from all board schools (*i.e.*, School Expulsion or Board Expulsion);

(iii) information about the school or program for expelled pupils to which the pupil is assigned; and

(iv) information about the right to appeal the expulsion, including steps that must be taken in this regard.[101]

---

[96] *Ibid.*, s. 311.4(2).
[97] *Ibid.*, s. 311.4(4).
[98] *Ibid.*, s. 311.4(3).
[99] *Ibid.*, s. 311.5.
[100] *Ibid.*, s. 311.6(1).

12. Expulsion Appeal Process

Both School Expulsions and Board Expulsions can be appealed to the tribunal designated to hear such appeals, being the Child and Family Services Review Board (hereafter the "CFSRB").[102] The procedures surrounding expulsion appeals are now found in section 311.7 of the *Education Act*. These provisions replace the procedures found in section 69.1 of Regulation 70 to the *Child and Family Services Act* ("O. Reg. 70") which have been repealed effective February 1, 2007.[103]

(a) Who may Appeal?

A board's decision to expel a pupil can be appealed by the following persons: (i) the parent or guardian unless the pupil is at least 18 years old or 16 or 17 years old and has withdrawn from parental control; (ii) a pupil who is at least 18 years old or 16 or 17 years old and has withdrawn from parental control; or (iii) such other persons as may be specified by the designated tribunal.[104]

(b) Notice of Appeal

The person entitled to Appeal (hereinafter the "Appellant") must give the CFSRB written notice of appeal within 30 days[105] after having been considered to receive notice of the decision.[106] The CFSRB may extend the time period for giving notice if there are reasonable grounds for the extension.[107]

The Notice of Appeal must:

(i) set out the date of the decision being appealed;
(ii) set out the name of the board that made the decision;
(iii) state whether the decision expels the pupil from his or her school or from all board schools;

---

[101] *Ibid.*, s. 311.6(2).
[102] *Ibid.*, s. 311.7, O. Reg. 472/07, ss. 1, 4.
[103] O. Reg. 537/07.
[104] *Education Act*, s. 311.7(2).
[105] Section 69.1(2) of O. Reg. 70 permitted an Appellant 60 days within which to provide the Notice of Appeal, but as indicated, this section was repealed by O. Reg. 537/07.
[106] See *Education Act*, s. 311.6(1) which requires a board that expels a pupil to give written notice promptly to all parties and to the pupil (if not a party to the expulsion hearing).
[107] O. Reg. 472/07, s. 5(2).

(iv) be in a form acceptable to the designated tribunal.[108]

The CFSRB cannot refuse to deal with an appeal on the ground that there is a deficiency in the content or form of the notice of appeal.[109]

(c) Parties to the Expulsion Appeal

The parties to the appeal are the following: (i) the board; (ii) the pupil if the pupil is at least 18 years old or 16 or 17 years old and has withdrawn from parental control; (iii) the parent or guardian, if he or she appealed the decision; and (iv) the person who appealed the decision to expel the pupil, if the decision was appealed by a person other than the pupil or the pupil's parent or guardian.[110]

(d) Hearing of Appeal

The CFSRB is required to commence a hearing within 30 days after receiving a written notice of appeal.[111] This time period may be extended by the CFSRB at the request of any party either before or after the period has expired.[112]

The expelled pupil has the right to be present at the appeal and to make a statement on his or her behalf, regardless of whether the pupil is a party to the appeal.[113]

(e) Powers of Designated Tribunal

After hearing an appeal, the CFSRB must do one of the following:

(i) Confirm the board's decision to expel (in the case of either a School Expulsion or a Board Expulsion).

(ii) Quash the expulsion and reinstate the pupil to the pre-expulsion school (in the case of either a School Expulsion or a Board Expulsion).

(iii) Change a Board Expulsion to a School Expulsion.[114]

The EAA further specifies that if the CFSRB either changes a Board Expulsion to a School Expulsion, or quashes an expulsion and reinstates

---

[108] O. Reg. 472/07, s. 5(3).
[109] O. Reg. 472/07, s. 5(4).
[110] *Education Act*, s. 311.7(4).
[111] O. Reg. 472/07, s. 6(1).
[112] O. Reg. 472/07, s. 6(2).
[113] O. Reg. 472/07, s. 6(3).
[114] O. Reg. 472/07, s. 6(4).

the pupil can order that any record of the expulsion be expunged or amended if appropriate.[115]

The EAA does not, however, address what happens to the pupil if the CFSRB changes a Board Expulsion to a School Expulsion. In the usual course where a School Expulsion is imposed by the school board at an expulsion hearing, the board committee will immediately transfer the pupil to a different school within the board. Neither the EAA or its regulations address such a transfer in the expulsion appeal context. The CFSRB does not have an explicit power to transfer the pupil; therefore, it remains to be seen how the CFSRB will interpret its powers in this regard.

(f) Decision of Tribunal

The CFSRB is required to provide each party, or counsel or agent with:

   (a) its decision on the appeal within 10 days after completing the hearing; and,

   (b) written reasons within 30 days after completing the hearing.[116]

The decision of the CFSRB is final.[117]

(g) Ministry Regulations regarding Expulsion Appeals

The Ministry of Education is empowered to make regulations: (i) designating a tribunal to hear appeals; (ii) prescribing procedures to be followed on an appeal; and (iii) prescribing the powers and duties of the designated tribunal.[118] To date, the only regulation passed under this section is O. Reg. 472/07, as discussed above. This regulation does not set out precise procedures to be followed, aside from the general guidelines discussed above. No further regulations have been passed to date.

Under the Safe Schools Regime, the CFSRB created its own Rules of Procedure and created forms for use in the expulsion appeal process. At the time of the writing of this text, the CFSRB was continuing to use the same Rules of Procedure and the same forms as those being used under the Safe Schools Regime; however, we understand that following the implementation of the new legislation there may be changes to the Rules of Procedure and/or forms.

---

[115] O. Reg. 472/07, s. 6(6).
[116] O. Reg. 472/07, s. 6(5). NOTE: Previously the tribunal was required to provide a copy of its decision within 10 days of completion of the expulsion appeal under subsection 69.1(9) of O. Reg. 70 (repealed effective February 1, 2007).
[117] *Education Act*, s. 311.7(5).
[118] *Ibid.*, s. 311.7(6).

F. EDUCATION OF SUSPENDED AND EXPELLED PUPILS

1. Overview

Under the EAA, school boards are required to provide at least one program for suspended pupils and at least one program for expelled pupils, in accordance with policies and guidelines issued by the Minister.[119]

On August 23, 2007, the Ministry of Education released Policy/Program Memorandum No. 141 ("PPM 141" in Appendix B) entitled "School Board Programs for Students on Long-Term Suspension", and Policy/ Program Memorandum No. 142 entitled "School Board Programs for Expelled Students" ("PPM 142" in Appendix C) which set out detailed requirements regarding these education programs. The Ministry of Education also announced funding to school boards for both of these programs, whereas previously only "strict discipline programs" for students under full expulsions were funded.[120] It is expected that the success of the new programs will be largely dependent on the adequacy of the Ministry funding and resources made available to boards in this regard.

2. Board Policies regarding Education Programs

PPMs 141 and 142 require school boards to develop policies regarding the operation of their programs for suspended and expelled pupils. At a minimum, the policies must address: (1) the discipline of pupils in the programs for unacceptable behaviour; and (2) measures taken to ensure a safe learning environment. The PPMs require that the policies be developed in consultation with a number of groups[121] and provide that boards must consider the needs of the individual student by showing sensitivity to diversity and cultural needs.[122] Therefore, school boards are

---

[119] *Ibid.*, s. 312(1).

[120] Programs for suspended pupils or those under limited expulsions were dependant on limited school board funding and restricted availability within the particular boards.

[121] Specifically the PPMs require boards to consult with parents, principals, teachers, students, school councils, Parent Involvement Committee, Special Education Advisory Committee, community partners, social service agencies, members of Aboriginal communities and "those groups that are traditionally not consulted".

[122] The PPM also requires that the policies comply with relevant Ministry policies on antiracism and ethnocultural equity and antidiscrimination education and with the principles in the Ministry document *Ontario First Nation, Métis, and Inuit Educational Policy Framework, 2007*. In addition, the PPM states that Boards are required to adhere to the *Municipal Freedom of Information and Protection of Privacy Act*, the

now required to implement distinct safe schools policies for their education programs for disciplined pupils, consistent with the requirements of the PPMs.

3. Education of Pupils under Short-Term Suspension

Although boards are not required to provide formal programs for pupils suspended for five days or less, PPM 141 stipulates that boards "are expected to provide homework packages for these students to help ensure that they do not fall behind in their school work."[123]

Under the Safe Schools Regime, the protocol for providing homework to suspended students varied between school boards. The PPM clarifies that boards/schools should be providing homework packages to all pupils under suspension. Administrators should review their school boards' relevant policies and procedures to confirm the appropriate protocols in this regard.

4. Education of Pupils under Long-Term Suspension or Expulsion

School boards are required to provide education programs for pupils under suspension for over 5 days in length ("Long-Term Suspensions") or under a Board Expulsion.[124] The PPMs stipulate that these programs can be offered through agreement with other boards; however, they note that any such agreements must respect collective agreements. The PPMs further specify that the delivery of such programs may take: "many forms, ranging from homework packages to attendance in a designated location at the board's discretion,"[125] which allows boards some flexibility regarding the provision of these education programs. In any event, PPM 141 requires

---

Ontario *Human Rights Code*, and the *Education Act* and its regulations and recommend that boards consult with legal counsel and freedom of information coordinators to ensure they meet their obligations.

[123] Policy/Program Memorandum No. 141 of the Minister of Education regarding "School Board Programs for Students on Long-Term Suspension" (PPM No. 141 in Appendix B).

[124] As indicated above, students given a "School Expulsion" are placed in another board school at the conclusion of the expulsion hearing.

[125] Policy/Program Memorandum No. 141 of the Minister of Education regarding "School Board Programs for Students on Long-Term Suspension" (PPM No. 141 in Appendix B).

that "[i]n all cases, every effort must be made to maintain the student's regular academic course work throughout the suspension period."[126]

Boards are required to develop a Student Action Plan ("SAP") for these pupils. In the case of expelled pupils and those suspended for more than 10 days, the SAP must include both an academic and non-academic component. The development of the SAP requires a "Planning Meeting" between school staff, family, and others where appropriate. In the case of expelled pupils, the SAP must be reviewed regularly to assess the pupil's progress. Before returning to school (after discipline is served and any requirements for a return to school have been met), a "Re-Entry" meeting must be held. The Re-Entry Process following an expulsion also requires the development of a "Re-Entry Plan" that includes: (1) a description of the re-entry process for successful transition back to school; and (2) identification of both academic and other supports required to sustain student learning. The PPMs also require that homework be given to pupils until the SAP is put into place.

5. Return to School after Completion of Program

The EAA clarifies the status of pupils under expulsion and addresses an expelled pupil's return to school. A pupil attending a program for expelled pupils offered by the pupil's board or through an agreement with another board remains the pupil of the expelling board unless: (i) the pupil is assigned to a program for expelled pupils but fails to attend; or (ii) the pupil registers as a pupil at another board.[127]

If a pupil expelled from one board registers as a pupil at a different board, the board may: (i) assign the pupil to one of its schools; or (ii) assign the pupil to an expelled pupil program, unless the pupil meets the requirements to return to school.[128]

If a board unknowingly assigns an expelled pupil to one of its schools and later learns of the expulsion, the board may remove the pupil from school and assign the pupil to a program for expelled pupils if: (1) the board does so promptly upon learning of the expulsion; and (ii) the pupil is not entitled to return to school.[129]

---

[126] Policy/Program Memorandum No. 141 of the Minister of Education regarding "School Board Programs for Students on Long-Term Suspension" (PPM No. 141 in Appendix B).
[127] *Education Act*, ss. 313(1) and (2).
[128] *Ibid.*, s. 314(1).
[129] *Ibid.*, s. 314(2).

A pupil under Board Expulsion is entitled to be readmitted to a board school if the pupil has either successfully completed a program for expelled pupils or satisfied the objectives for the successful completion of such a program, as determined by a person who provides an expelled pupil program.[130]

An expelled pupil who has successfully completed the program may apply in writing to a person designated by the board to be readmitted to a school of the board, and the board must readmit the pupil to a school of the board and must promptly inform the pupil in writing of the readmittance.[131]

Once a pupil has completed an expelled pupil program, a board cannot require the pupil to attend another such program or refuse to admit the pupil on the basis that the program completed by the pupil was offered by another board or another person.[132]

The EAA permits a pupil who was given a School Expulsion to apply in writing to a person designated by the board to be re-assigned to the school from which he or she was expelled.[133] There is no corresponding requirement on the board, however, to place the pupil in the school. The EAA further states that nothing in this Part requires a board to admit or readmit a pupil not otherwise qualified to be a resident pupil of the board.[134]

A school board faced with a written request by a pupil (given a School Expulsion) to be re-assigned to his or her pre-expulsion school should consider the request and make a determination in all of the circumstances as to whether the pupil should be placed in that school. Factors such as any existing bail conditions that preclude the pupil from attending at that particular school would, of course, prevent a board from re-admitting the pupil to the school. Other factors such as the safety of those involved in the incident that lead to the expulsion should be considered prior to re-admitting the pupil.

Principals should also reference any school board policies, procedures or protocols that address a pupil's return to school following expulsion.

---

[130] *Ibid.*, s. 314.1.
[131] *Ibid.*, s. 314.1(3).
[132] *Ibid.*, s. 314.2.
[133] *Ibid.*, s. 314.3.
[134] *Ibid.*, s. 314.4.

G. TRANSITIONAL PROVISIONS

The EAA sets out various transition provisions that address how to deal with expulsions that were imposed under the *Safe Schools Act*, but remain outstanding on February 1, 2008.

1. Limited Expulsions

In the case of pupils serving limited expulsions on February 1, 2008, the board must: (i) assign the pupil to a board school and offer a plan to assist the pupil's transition back to school; or (ii) assign the pupil to a program for expelled pupils.[135] If the pupil is assigned to a program for expelled pupils, the pupil is not entitled to attend school until the date on which he or she would have been entitled to return to school under subsection 309(14) of the old *Education Act* provisions.[136]

2. Full Expulsions

In the case of pupils serving full expulsions on February 1, 2008, the board must reassign the pupil to a program for expelled pupils and the pupil will be entitled to return to school in accordance with the EAA provisions and sections 314.1 and 314.2 apply (with modifications as required).[137]

H. DENIAL OF ACCESS PROVISIONS

The *Safe Schools Act* gave principals[138] the power to deny access to a person whose presence "is detrimental to the safety or well-being of a person on the premises." Since the term "person" specifically made reference to a "pupil"[139] it was clear that principals could deny access to pupils. The power was found in section 305 of the *Education Act* and Regulation 474/00 to the *Education Act* (hereinafter "O. Reg. 474/00").

A similar power is found in *Education Act* section 265(1)(m), which requires a principal to "refuse to admit to the school or classroom a person whose presence in the school or classroom would in the principal's judgment be detrimental to the physical or mental well-being of the

---

[135] *Ibid.*, s. 314.8(1).
[136] Ibid., s. 314.8(2).
[137] Ibid., s. 314.9.
[138] O. Reg. 474/00 also gave this power to a vice-principal and "another person authorized by the board to make such a determination."
[139] O. Reg. 474/00, s. 2(1).

pupils." The test in this section is slightly different than under section 305/O. Reg. 474/00[140] and this section provides for an appeal to the full board of trustees, whereas there is no right to appeal under section 305/O. Reg. 474/00.

Notably, in addition to the powers to discipline and exclude pupils, is a school board's power to transfer a pupil to a different school within the board.[141] The Ontario Divisional Court recently upheld the transfer of two pupils in a situation involving safety concerns. In *K.B. (Litigation Guardian of) v. Toronto District School Board*,[142] the Divisional Court confirmed that a student does not have the right to attend a particular school and held that in the circumstances of this case, a school board has the power to transfer pupils. See Appendix G, for a detailed summary of the facts in this case.

1. Removal of Application to Pupils

In August 2007, the Minister of Education filed Regulation 471/07 ("O. Reg. 471/07") to amend O. Reg. 474/00 to the effect that the denial of access provisions in section 305/O. Reg. 474 are not applicable to pupils enrolled in the school, or pupils attending a program for disciplined pupils on the school premises.[143] Given that principals no longer have the power to deny access to enrolled pupils, the only comparable option that remains is the power to exclude a pupil under subsection 265(1)(m), which has not been frequently used in the past. The power to transfer pupils was not impacted by the legislative changes.

---

[140] Specifically, the test in O. Reg. 474/00 refers to the safety or well-being of "a person on the premises" whereas subsection 265(1)(m) refers to the "physical or mental well-being of the pupils".

[141] In certain circumstances, it may be necessary to transfer a student, for example, where a student is charged with a criminal offence and prohibited by bail conditions from attending at a particular school. There may also be other circumstances where such a transfer is deemed necessary for safety reasons.

[142] [2008] O.J. No. 475 (Ont. Div. Ct.). The author acted as co-counsel to the Respondents in this case.

[143] The Regulation also provides that if on January 31, 2008 a pupil continues to be denied access to school premises and was a pupil at the time of the denial of access, as of February 1, 2008, the pupil will be entitled to be on school premises in accordance with the Regulation.

2. Implications regarding Pupils with Special Needs

In the past, the denial of access provisions in section 305/O. Reg. 474/00 were sometimes used to deny or limit access to students with special needs in cases involving significant safety concerns. The application of these provisions and section 265(1)(m) to special education pupils was, in fact, sanctioned by the Ontario Court of Appeal in the decision of *Bonnah (Litigation Guardian of) v. Ottawa-Carleton District School Board*[144] (hereinafter "Bonnah"). The Court of Appeal held that any interpretation which were to exclude the application of these provisions to exceptional pupils could: "seriously imperil the safety of exceptional pupils and others."

As indicated, subsequent to *Bonnah*, O. Reg. 474/00 was amended to specifically remove the application of section 305/O. Reg. 474/00 to pupils. The effect of this amendment is that the reasoning in *Bonnah* regarding the application of section 305/O. Reg. 474/00 to pupils is no longer applicable; however, this leaves intact the *Bonnah* reasoning as it pertains to subsection 265(1)(m).

In *Bonnah*, the Ontario Court of Appeal considered a situation where the education of a special needs pupil conflicted with maintaining a safe school environment. The Court of Appeal set out steps which a school board could follow if faced with the situation where a special needs pupil raises safety concerns in a particular placement.

Essentially the Court of Appeal held that where a special needs pupil raises genuine safety concerns, the school can offer to transfer the pupil to an alternate placement where the safety concerns do not arise. If the parents refuse the transfer, the school cannot unilaterally transfer the pupil, because the comprehensive scheme for special needs placements set out in the *Education Act* must be followed.[145] The school can, however, exclude the pupil from the classroom or the school, to the extent that this may be necessary for genuine safety reasons. The Court of Appeal stipulated; however, that the principal's response to the safety concerns must be reasonable and that the principal "must bear in mind the special significance of the placement decision as it relates to exceptional pupils and strive to minimize any interference with that placement."[146] As

---

[144] [2003] O.J. No. 1156, 64 O.R. (3d) 454 (Ont. C.A.).
[145] In the *Bonnah* situation, the parents had appealed an IPRC decision to change the pupil's placement, and section 20 of O. Reg. 181/98 to the *Education Act* provides that the pupil's original placement is stayed (*i.e.*, it cannot be altered) pending the placement appeal.
[146] *Bonnah (Litigation Guardian of) v. Ottawa-Carleton District School Board*, [2003] O.J. No. 1156, 64 O.R. (3d) 454 (Ont. C.A.) at para. 36.

indicated, this analysis and reasoning still applies in the context of section 265(1)(m). Notably, the Court of Appeal, in its decision, confirms the paramount importance of maintaining a safe school environment.

In any event, it remains to be seen how the removal of the application of section 305/O. Reg. 474/00 to enrolled pupils will impact on how administrators address serious safety concerns in their schools, particularly those involving pupils with special needs.

Matters involving safety issues and special needs pupils have been drawing increasing legal attention. In recent years, there has been an increase in work refusals by school staff working with special needs pupils who pose safety risks.[147] As a result, in Ontario, the Ministry of Labour has become heavily involved with these issues, and various investigators have issued broad-reaching orders against school boards in this regard.

In addition, issues have arisen regarding the potential liability of school boards for injuries to staff caused by special needs pupils. For example, in the Saskatchewan Court of Appeal decision of *Kendal v. St. Paul's Roman Catholic Separate School Division No. 20*,[148] a special needs teacher sought damages from her employer school board for injuries she suffered when she was struck by a special needs pupil. The Court of Appeal upheld the trial judge's decision which found that the safety risk to the teacher did not outweigh the social value of offering this program, and that the school board had recognized the risks and had taken steps to ameliorate them.

I. DISCIPLINE OF PUPILS WITH SPECIAL NEEDS

See also above under Heading C.2.(c), "Progressive Discipline involving Students with Special Needs".

The issue of the application of the student discipline provisions to special needs pupils is a difficult one that requires significant consideration by administrators confronted with this challenging issue.

The EAA has added many more factors that administrators are now required to consider before imposing discipline, particularly in cases of pupils with special needs. Further, as explained above, interventions, supports and consequences for pupils with special education needs must be "consistent with the student's strengths, needs, goals, and expectations

---

[147] Workplace safety provisions that were traditionally used to address safety concerns regarding the physical surroundings of the workplace are now being applied in the context of individuals in the workplace who are deemed to present a safety risk. (In Ontario, see section 43, *Occupational Health and Safety Act*, R.S.O. 1990, c. O.1.).

[148] [2004] S.J. No. 361 (Sask. C.A.).

contained in his or her Individual Education Plan (IEP)." Essentially, principals must accommodate pupils with special needs in the discipline process, as has always been required under the Ontario *Human Rights Code*. In addition, principals must now specifically consider the student's strengths, needs, goals and expectations as set out in the pupil's IEP when implementing a progressive discipline approach to misconduct by students with special needs.

Of course, as in all cases, administrators should be considering creative and effective progressive discipline interventions. This is particularly the case regarding pupils with special needs. It is even more important to take a pro-active, creative approach to dealing with student misconduct than ever before. Appropriate supports should be in place to address possible safety concerns and to focus on the prevention of such incidents. In the event that other options are exhausted and the principal is required to consider more traditional discipline, principals will have the following two options: (1) suspension or expulsion, or (2) excluding the pupil under section 265(1)(m), which gives rise to an appeal to a full board of trustees, since denial of access provisions are no longer available in respect of pupils.

Before imposing traditional discipline; however, administrators should carefully consider all of the mitigating or other factors. Administrators should review applicable school board policies and procedures regarding the imposition of discipline on special needs pupils, and should consult with their Supervisory Officers or other relevant resources, and/or legal counsel in this regard. As indicated above, principals should confer with the pupil's teachers and persons with special education expertise in order to make informed decisions regarding these matters.

It is expected that there will be continued conflict in cases where discipline is applied to pupils with special needs. Further, the explicit incorporation of human rights concepts in the mitigating factors may give rise to increased human rights complaints in this context.

LEGISLATION

EDUCATION ACT

R.S.O. 1990, c. E.2

Amendments to Part XIII: Original provisions for Part XIII repealed S.O. 1997, c. 31, ss. 128, 129; new provisions S.O. 2000, c. 12, s. 3, in force September 1, 2000, except s. 3 enacting ss. 306-308 and 309-311, in force September 1, 2001; new provisions S.O. 2007, c. 14, ss. 1-6, in force February 1, 2008.

Part XIII
Behaviour, Discipline and Safety

300. (1) **Interpretation** — In this Part,

"school premises" means, with respect to a school, the school buildings and premises.

(2) **Same** — In this Part, where reference is made to a regulation or to a matter prescribed by regulation, it means a regulation to be made by the Minister under this Part.
[S.O. 2000, c. 12, s. 3, in force September 1, 2000]

(3) **Receipt of notice** — Where notice is given to a person under this Part, it shall be considered to have been received by the person in accordance with the following rules:

1. If the notice is sent by mail or another method in which an original document is sent, the notice shall be considered to have been received by the person to whom it was sent on the fifth school day after the day on which it was sent.
2. If the notice is sent by fax or another method of electronic transmission, the notice shall be considered to have been received by the person to whom it was sent on the first school day after the day on which it was sent.

[S.O. 2007, c. 14, s. 1, in force February 1, 2008]

301. (1) **Provincial code of conduct** — The Minister may establish a code of conduct governing the behaviour of all persons in schools.

(2) **Purposes** — The following are the purposes of the code of conduct:

1. To ensure that all members of the school community, especially people in positions of authority, are treated with respect and dignity.
2. To promote responsible citizenship by encouraging appropriate participation in the civic life of the school community.

3. To maintain an environment where conflict and difference can be addressed in a manner characterized by respect and civility.
4. To encourage the use of non-violent means to resolve conflict.
5. To promote the safety of people in the schools.
6. To discourage the use of alcohol and illegal drugs.

(3) **Notice** — Every board shall take such steps as the Minister directs to bring the code of conduct to the attention of pupils, parents and guardians of pupils and others who may be present in schools under the jurisdiction of the board.

(4) **Code is policy** — The code of conduct is a policy of the Minister.

(5) **Policies and guidelines governing conduct** — The Minister may establish additional policies and guidelines with respect to the conduct of persons in schools.

(6) **Same, governing discipline** — The Minister may establish policies and guidelines with respect to disciplining pupils, specifying, for example, the circumstances in which a pupil is subject to discipline and the forms and the extent of discipline that may be imposed in particular circumstances.
[S.O. 2000, c. 12, s. 3, in force September 1, 2000]

(6.1) **Same, procedural matters** — The Minister may establish policies and guidelines with respect to,
(a) appeals of a decision to suspend a pupil;
(b) principals' investigations to determine whether to recommend that a pupil be expelled; and
(c) expulsion hearings.
[S.O. 2007, c. 14, s. 2, in force February 1, 2008]

(7) **Same, promoting safety** — The Minister may establish policies and guidelines to promote the safety of pupils.

(8) **Different policies, etc.** — The Minister may establish different policies and guidelines under this section for different circumstances, for different locations and for different classes of persons.

(9) **Duty of boards** — The Minister may require boards to comply with policies and guidelines established under this section.
[S.O. 2007, c. 12, s. 3, in force September 1, 2000]

(10) **Not regulations** — Policies and guidelines established under this section are not regulations within the meaning of Part III (Regulations) of the *Legislation Act, 2006*.
[S.O. 2000, c. 12, s. 3, in force September 1, 2000; S.O. 2006, c. 21, Sched. F, s. 136(1), in force July 25, 2007]

302. (1) **Board's policies and guidelines governing conduct** — Every board shall establish policies and guidelines with respect to the conduct of persons in schools within the board's jurisdiction and the policies and guidelines must address such matters and include such requirements as the Minister may specify.

(2) **Same, governing discipline** — A board may establish policies and guidelines with respect to disciplining pupils, and the policies and guidelines must be consistent with this Part and with the policies and guidelines established by the Minister under section 301, and must address such matters and include such requirements as the Minister may specify.

(3) **Same, promoting safety** — If required to do so by the Minister, a board shall establish policies and guidelines to promote the safety of pupils, and the policies and guidelines must be consistent with those established by the Minister under section 301 and must address such matters and include such requirements as the Minister may specify.

(4) **Same, governing access to school premises** — A board may establish policies and guidelines governing access to school premises, and the policies and guidelines must be consistent with the regulations made under section 305 and must address such matters and include such requirements as the Minister may specify.

(5) **Same, governing appropriate dress** — If required to do so by the Minister, a board shall establish policies and guidelines respecting appropriate dress for pupils in schools within the board's jurisdiction, and the policies and guidelines must address such matters and include such requirements as the Minister may specify.
[S.O. 2000, c. 12, s. 3, in force September 1, 2000]

(6) **Same, procedural matters** — A board shall establish policies and guidelines governing,
- (a) appeals of a decision to suspend a pupil;
- (b) principals' investigations to determine whether to recommend that a pupil be expelled; and
- (c) expulsion hearings.

[S.O. 2007, c. 14, s. 3(1), in force February 1, 2008]

(6.1) **Same** — If the Minister has established policies and guidelines under subsection 301 (6.1), a board's policies and guidelines under subsection (6) must address such matters and include such requirements as specified by the Minister.
[S.O. 2007, c. 14, s. 3(1), in force February 1, 2008]

(7) **Different policies, etc.** — A board may establish different policies and guidelines under this section for different circumstances, for different locations and for different classes of persons.

(8) Role of school councils — When establishing policies and guidelines under this section, a board shall consider the views of school councils with respect to the contents of the policies and guidelines.

(9) Periodic review — The board shall periodically review its policies and guidelines established under this section and shall solicit the views of pupils, teachers, staff, volunteers working in the schools, parents and guardians, school councils and the public.
[S.O. 2000, c. 12, s. 3, in force September 1, 2000]

(9.1) Communication of policies — A board shall ensure that a copy of the policies and guidelines it establishes under subsections (1) and (2) are available to the public.
[S.O. 2007, c. 14, s. 3(2), in force February 1, 2008]

(10) Not regulations — Policies and guidelines established under this section are not regulations within the meaning of Part III (Regulations) of the *Legislation Act, 2006*.
[S.O. 2000, c. 12, s. 3, in force September 1, 2000; S.O. 2006, c. 21, Sched. F, s. 136 (1), in force July 25, 2007]

303. (1) **Local codes of conduct** — A board may direct the principal of a school to establish a local code of conduct governing the behaviour of all persons in the school, and the local code must be consistent with the provincial code established under subsection 301 (1) and must address such matters and include such requirements as the board may specify.

(2) **Same, mandatory** — A board shall direct a principal to establish a local code of conduct if the board is required to do so by the Minister, and the local code must address such matters and include such requirements as the Minister may specify.

(3) **Role of school council** — When establishing or reviewing a local code of conduct, the principal shall consider the views of the school council with respect to its contents.
[S.O. 2000, c. 12, s. 3, in force September 1, 2000]

(4) **Not regulation** — A local code of conduct is not a regulation within the meaning of Part III (Regulations) of the *Legislation Act, 2006*.
[S.O. 2000, c. 12, s. 3, in force September 1, 2000; S.O. 2006, c. 21, Sched. F, s. 136 (1), in force July 25, 2007]

304. (1) **Opening and closing exercises at schools** — Every board shall ensure that opening or closing exercises are held in each school under the board's jurisdiction, in accordance with the requirements set out in the regulations.

(2) **Same** — The opening or closing exercises must include the singing of *O Canada* and may include the recitation of a pledge of citizenship in the form set out in the regulations.

(3) **Exceptions** — A pupil is not required to participate in the opening or closing exercises in such circumstances as are prescribed by regulation.

305. (1) **Access to school premises** — The Minister may make regulations governing access to school premises, specifying classes of persons who are permitted to be on school premises and specifying the days and times at which different classes of persons are prohibited from being on school premises.

(2) **Prohibition** — No person shall enter or remain on school premises unless he or she is authorized by regulation to be there on that day or at that time.

(3) **Same, board policy** — A person shall not enter or remain on school premises if he or she is prohibited under a board policy from being there on that day or at that time.

(4) **Direction to leave** — The principal of a school may direct a person to leave the school premises if the principal believes that the person is prohibited by regulation or under a board policy from being there.

(5) **Offence** — Every person who contravenes subsection (2) is guilty of an offence.
[S.O. 2000, c. 12, s. 3, in force September 1, 2000]

Suspension

306. (1) **Activities leading to possible suspension** — A principal shall consider whether to suspend a pupil if he or she believes that the pupil has engaged in any of the following activities while at school, at a school-related activity or in other circumstances where engaging in the activity will have an impact on the school climate:

1. Uttering a threat to inflict serious bodily harm on another person.
2. Possessing alcohol or illegal drugs.
3. Being under the influence of alcohol.
4. Swearing at a teacher or at another person in a position of authority.
5. Committing an act of vandalism that causes extensive damage to school property at the pupil's school or to property located on the premises of the pupil's school.
6. Bullying.
7. Any other activity that is an activity for which a principal may suspend a pupil under a policy of the board.

[S.O. 2007, c. 14, s. 4, in force February 1, 2008]

(2) **Factors principal must consider** — In considering whether to suspend a pupil for engaging in an activity described in subsection (1), a

principal shall take into account any mitigating or other factors prescribed by the regulations.
[S.O. 2007, c. 14, s. 4, in force February 1, 2008]

(3) **Suspension** — If a principal decides to suspend a pupil for engaging in an activity described in subsection (1), the principal shall suspend the pupil from his or her school and from engaging in all school-related activities.
[S.O. 2007, c. 14, s. 4, in force February 1, 2008]

(4) **Duration of suspension** — A suspension under this section shall be for no less than one school day and no more than 20 school days and, in considering how long the suspension should be, a principal shall take into account any mitigating or other factors prescribed by the regulations.
[S.O. 2007, c. 14, s. 4, in force February 1, 2008]

(5) **Assignment to program, etc.** — When a principal suspends a pupil under this section, he or she shall assign the pupil to a program for suspended pupils in accordance with any policies or guidelines issued by the Minister.
[S.O. 2007, c. 14, s. 4, in force February 1, 2008]

(6) **Policies and guidelines** — The Minister may issue policies and guidelines to boards to assist principals in interpreting and administering this section.
[S.O. 2007, c. 14, s. 4, in force February 1, 2008]

(7) **School-related activities** — A pupil who is suspended is not considered to be engaged in school-related activities by virtue of participating in a program for suspended pupils.
[S.O. 2007, c. 14, s. 4, in force February 1, 2008]

307. Only one suspension per occurrence — A principal may not suspend a pupil under section 306 more than once for the same occurrence.
[S.O. 2007, c. 14, s. 4, in force February 1, 2008]

308. (1) **Notice of suspension** — A principal who suspends a pupil under section 306 shall,
- (a) inform the pupil's teacher of the suspension; and
- (b) make all reasonable efforts to inform the pupil's parent or guardian of the suspension within 24 hours of the suspension being imposed, unless,
  - (i) the pupil is at least 18 years old, or
  - (ii) the pupil is 16 or 17 years old and has withdrawn from parental control.

[S.O. 2007, c. 14, s. 4, in force February 1, 2008]

(2) **Same** — A principal who suspends a pupil under section 306 shall ensure that written notice of the suspension is given promptly to the following persons:
1. The pupil.
2. The pupil's parent or guardian, unless,
    i. the pupil is at least 18 years old, or
    ii. the pupil is 16 or 17 years old and has withdrawn from parental control.
3. Such other persons as may be specified by board policy.

[S.O. 2007, c. 14, s. 4, in force February 1, 2008]

(3) **Contents of notice** — The notice under subsection (2) must include the following:
1. The reason for the suspension.
2. The duration of the suspension.
3. Information about any program for suspended pupils to which the pupil is assigned.
4. Information about the right to appeal the suspension under section 309, including,
    i. a copy of the board policies and guidelines governing the appeal established by the board under subsection 302 (6), and
    ii. the name and contact information of the supervisory officer to whom notice of the appeal must be given under subsection 309 (2).

[S.O. 2007, c. 14, s. 4, in force February 1, 2008]

309. (1) **Appeal of suspension** — The following persons may appeal, to the board, a principal's decision to suspend a pupil under section 306:
1. The pupil's parent or guardian, unless,
    i. the pupil is at least 18 years old, or
    ii. the pupil is 16 or 17 years old and has withdrawn from parental control.
2. The pupil, if,
    i. the pupil is at least 18 years old, or
    ii. the pupil is 16 or 17 years old and has withdrawn from parental control.
3. Such other persons as may be specified by board policy.

[S.O. 2007, c. 14, s. 4, in force February 1, 2008]

(2) **Board designate** — Every board shall designate a supervisory officer for the purposes of receiving notices of intention to appeal a suspension.

[S.O. 2007, c. 14, s. 4, in force February 1, 2008]

(3) Notice of appeal — A person who is entitled to appeal a suspension under subsection (1) must give written notice of his or her intention to appeal to the supervisory officer designated by the board within 10 school days of the commencement of the suspension.
[S.O. 2007, c. 14, s. 4, in force February 1, 2008]

(4) Board to inform all parties — After receiving a notice of intention to appeal under subsection (3), the board shall promptly contact every person entitled to appeal the suspension under subsection (1) and inform him or her that it has received the notice of intention to appeal.
[S.O. 2007, c. 14, s. 4, in force February 1, 2008]

(5) Party may contact supervisory officer — A person who has given notice of intention to appeal under subsection (3) may contact the supervisory officer designated under subsection (2) to discuss any matter respecting the appeal of the suspension and, for the purposes of this section, the supervisory officer has the powers and duties set out in board policy.
[S.O. 2007, c. 14, s. 4, in force February 1, 2008]

(6) Hearing of appeal — The board shall hear and determine the appeal within 15 school days of receiving notice under subsection (3), unless the parties agree on a later deadline, and shall not refuse to deal with the appeal on the ground that there is a deficiency in the notice of appeal.
[S.O. 2007, c. 14, s. 4, in force February 1, 2008]

(7) Appeal process — Subject to this section, an appeal shall be conducted in accordance with the requirements established by board policy.
[S.O. 2007, c. 14, s. 4, in force February 1, 2008]

(8) Parties to appeal — The parties to the appeal are:
1. The principal who suspended the pupil.
2. The pupil, if,
    i. the pupil is at least 18 years old, or
    ii. the pupil is 16 or 17 years old and has withdrawn from parental control.
3. The pupil's parent or guardian, if the pupil's parent or guardian appealed the decision to suspend the pupil.
4. The person who appealed the decision to suspend the pupil, if the decision was appealed by a person other than the pupil or the pupil's parent or guardian.
5. Such other persons as may be specified by board policy.

[S.O. 2007, c. 14, s. 4, in force February 1, 2008]

(9) **Pupil may attend** — A pupil who is not a party to the appeal under subsection (8) has the right to be present at the appeal and to make a statement on his or her own behalf. 2007, c. 14, s. 4.
[S.O. 2007, c. 14, s. 4, in force February 1, 2008]

(10) **Powers on appeal** — The board shall,
(a) confirm the suspension and the duration of the suspension;
(b) confirm the suspension, but shorten its duration, even if the suspension that is under appeal has already been served, and order that the record of the suspension be amended accordingly; or
(c) quash the suspension and order that the record of the suspension be expunged, even if the suspension that is under appeal has already been served.
[S.O. 2007, c. 14, s. 4, in force February 1, 2008]

(11) **Decision final** — The decision of the board on an appeal under this section is final.
[S.O. 2007, c. 14, s. 4, in force February 1, 2008]

(12) **Committee** — The board may authorize a committee of at least three members of the board to exercise and perform powers and duties on behalf of the board under this section, and may impose conditions and restrictions on the committee.
[S.O. 2007, c. 14, s. 4, in force February 1, 2008]

Suspension, Investigation and Possible Expulsion

310. (1) **Activities leading to suspension** — A principal shall suspend a pupil if he or she believes that the pupil has engaged in any of the following activities while at school, at a school-related activity or in other circumstances where engaging in the activity will have an impact on the school climate:
1. Possessing a weapon, including possessing a firearm.
2. Using a weapon to cause or to threaten bodily harm to another person.
3. Committing physical assault on another person that causes bodily harm requiring treatment by a medical practitioner.
4. Committing sexual assault.
5. Trafficking in weapons or in illegal drugs.
6. Committing robbery.
7. Giving alcohol to a minor.
8. Any other activity that, under a policy of a board, is an activity for which a principal must suspend a pupil and, therefore in

accordance with this Part, conduct an investigation to determine whether to recommend to the board that the pupil be expelled.
[S.O. 2007, c. 14, s. 4, in force February 1, 2008]

(2) **Same** — A pupil who is suspended under this section is suspended from his or her school and from engaging in all school-related activities.
[S.O. 2007, c. 14, s. 4, in force February 1, 2008]

(3) **Duration of suspension** — A principal may suspend a pupil under this section for up to 20 school days and, in considering how long the suspension should be, the principal shall take into account any mitigating or other factors prescribed by the regulations.
[S.O. 2007, c. 14, s. 4, in force February 1, 2008]

(4) **Assignment to program, etc.** — When a principal suspends a pupil under this section, he or she shall assign the pupil to a program for suspended pupils in accordance with any policies or guidelines issued by the Minister.
[S.O. 2007, c. 14, s. 4, in force February 1, 2008]

311. (1) **Notice of suspension** — A principal who suspends a pupil under section 310 shall,
 (a) inform the pupil's teacher of the suspension; and
 (b) make all reasonable efforts to inform the pupil's parent or guardian of the suspension within 24 hours of the suspension being imposed, unless,
   (i) the pupil is at least 18 years old, or
   (ii) the pupil is 16 or 17 years old and has withdrawn from parental control.
[S.O. 2007, c. 14, s. 4, in force February 1, 2008]

(2) **Same** — A principal who suspends a pupil under section 310 shall ensure that written notice of the suspension is given promptly to the following persons:
 1. The pupil.
 2. The pupil's parent or guardian, unless,
   i. the pupil is at least 18 years old, or
   ii. the pupil is 16 or 17 years old and has withdrawn from parental control.
 3. Such other persons as may be specified by board policy.
[S.O. 2007, c. 14, s. 4, in force February 1, 2008]

(3) **Contents of notice** — The notice under subsection (2) must include the following:
 1. The reason for the suspension.
 2. The duration of the suspension.

3. Information about any program for suspended pupils to which the pupil is assigned.
4. Information about the investigation the principal will conduct under section 311.1 to determine whether to recommend that the pupil be expelled.
5. A statement indicating that,
    i. there is no immediate right to appeal the suspension,
    ii. if the principal does not recommend to the board that the pupil be expelled following the investigation under section 311.1, the suspension will become subject to appeal under section 311.2, and
    iii. if there is an expulsion hearing because the principal recommends to the board that the pupil be expelled, the suspension may be addressed by parties at the hearing.

[S.O. 2007, c. 14, s. 4, in force February 1, 2008]

311.1 (1) **Investigation following suspension** — When a pupil is suspended under section 310, the principal shall conduct an investigation to determine whether to recommend to the board that the pupil be expelled.
[S.O. 2007, c. 14, s. 4, in force February 1, 2008]

(2) **Conduct of investigation** — The principal's investigation shall begin promptly following the suspension and shall be conducted in accordance with the requirements established by board policy and, for the purpose of the investigation, the principal has the powers and duties set out in the policy.
[S.O. 2007, c. 14, s. 4, in force February 1, 2008]

(3) **Same** — As part of the investigation, the principal shall make all reasonable efforts to speak with the following persons:
1. The pupil.
2. The pupil's parent or guardian, unless,
    i. the pupil is at least 18 years old, or
    ii. the pupil is 16 or 17 years old and has withdrawn from parental control.
3. Any other person whom the principal has reason to believe may have relevant information.

[S.O. 2007, c. 14, s. 4, in force February 1, 2008]

(4) **Factors principal must consider** — In considering whether to recommend to the board that the pupil be expelled, a principal shall take into account any mitigating or other factors prescribed by the regulations.
[S.O. 2007, c. 14, s. 4, in force February 1, 2008]

(5) **If expulsion not recommended** — If, on concluding the investigation, the principal decides not to recommend to the board that the pupil be expelled, the principal shall,
   (a) confirm the suspension and the duration of the suspension;
   (b) confirm the suspension but shorten its duration, even if the suspension has already been served, and amend the record of the suspension accordingly; or
   (c) withdraw the suspension and expunge the record of the suspension, even if the suspension has already been served.
[S.O. 2007, c. 14, s. 4, in force February 1, 2008]

(6) **Same: notice** — If the principal does not recommend to the board that the pupil be expelled, the principal shall ensure that written notice containing the following information is given promptly to every person to whom he or she was required to give notice of the suspension under section 311:
1. A statement that the pupil will not be subject to an expulsion hearing for the activity that resulted in the suspension.
2. A statement indicating whether the principal has, under subsection (5), confirmed the suspension and its duration, confirmed the suspension but reduced its duration or withdrawn the suspension.
3. Unless the suspension was withdrawn, information about the right to appeal the suspension under section 311.2, including,
   i. a copy of the board policies and guidelines governing the appeal established by the board under subsection 302 (6), and
   ii. the name and contact information of the supervisory officer to whom notice of the appeal must be given under section 311.2.

[S.O. 2007, c. 14, s. 4, in force February 1, 2008]

(7) **If expulsion recommended: report** — If, on concluding the investigation, the principal decides to recommend to the board that the pupil be expelled, he or she shall prepare a report that contains the following:
1. A summary of the principal's findings.
2. The principal's recommendation as to whether the pupil should be expelled from his or her school only or from all schools of the board.
3. The principal's recommendation as to,
   i. the type of school that might benefit the pupil, if the pupil is expelled from his or her school only, or
   ii. the type of program for expelled pupils that might benefit the pupil, if the pupil is expelled from all schools of the board.

[S.O. 2007, c. 14, s. 4, in force February 1, 2008]

(8) **Same** — The principal shall promptly provide a copy of the report to the board and to every person whom the principal was required to give notice of the suspension under section 311.
[S.O. 2007, c. 14, s. 4, in force February 1, 2008]

(9) **Written notice** — The principal shall ensure that written notice containing the following is given to every person to whom the principal was required to give notice of the suspension under section 311 at the same time as the principal's report is provided to that person:
1. A statement that the pupil will be subject to an expulsion hearing for the activity that resulted in the suspension.
2. A copy of the board policies and guidelines governing the expulsion hearing established by the board under subsection 302 (6).
3. A statement that the person has the right to respond, in writing, to the principal's report provided under this section.
4. Detailed information about the procedures and possible outcomes of the expulsion hearing, including, but not limited to, information explaining that,
    i. if the board does not expel the pupil, it will, with respect to the suspension imposed under section 310, confirm the suspension, shorten its duration or withdraw it,
    ii. the parties will have the right to make submissions during the expulsion hearing as to whether, if the pupil is not expelled, the suspension imposed under section 310 should be confirmed, reduced or withdrawn,
    iii. any decision of the board with respect to the suspension imposed under section 310 made at the expulsion hearing is final and not subject to appeal,
    iv. if the board expels the pupil from his or her school only, the board will assign the pupil to another school, and
    v. if the board expels the pupil from all schools of the board, the board will assign the pupil to a program for expelled pupils.
5. The name and contact information of a supervisory officer whom the person may contact to discuss any matter respecting the expulsion hearing.

[S.O. 2007, c. 14, s. 4, in force February 1, 2008]

(10) **Party may respond** — A person who is entitled to receive the principal's report under subsection (8) and written notice under subsection (9) may respond, in writing, to the principal and the board.
[S.O. 2007, c. 14, s. 4, in force February 1, 2008]

311.2 Appeal of suspension — If the principal does not recommend to the board that the pupil be expelled and does not withdraw the suspension, the suspension may be appealed and section 309 applies for that purpose, with necessary modifications, subject to the following:
1. A person who is entitled to appeal must give written notice of his or her intention to appeal within five school days of the date on which he or she is considered, in accordance with the rules set out in subsection 300 (3), to have received the notice given under subsection 311.1 (9).
2. If the principal confirmed the suspension but reduced its duration under subsection 311.1 (8), the appeal is from the reduced suspension and not the original suspension.

[S.O. 2007, c. 14, s. 4, in force February 1, 2008]

311.3 (1) Expulsion hearing by board — If a principal recommends to the board that a pupil be expelled, the board shall hold an expulsion hearing and, for that purpose, the board has the powers and duties specified by board policy.

[S.O. 2007, c. 14, s. 4, in force February 1, 2008]

(2) **Conduct of hearing** — Subject to the requirements set out in this section, the expulsion hearing shall be conducted in accordance with the requirements established by board policy.

[S.O. 2007, c. 14, s. 4, in force February 1, 2008]

(3) **Parties** — The parties to the expulsion hearing are:
1. The principal.
2. The pupil, if,
    i. the pupil is at least 18 years old, or
    ii. the pupil is 16 or 17 years old and has withdrawn from parental control.
3. The pupil's parent or guardian, unless,
    i. the pupil is at least 18 years old, or
    ii. the pupil is 16 or 17 years old and has withdrawn from parental control.
4. Such other persons as may be specified by board policy.

[S.O. 2007, c. 14, s. 4, in force February 1, 2008]

(4) **Pupil may attend** — A pupil who is not a party to the expulsion hearing under subsection (3) has the right to be present at the hearing and to make a statement on his or her own behalf.

(5) **Submissions and views of parties** — At the hearing, the board shall,

(a) consider the submissions of each party in whatever form the party chooses to deliver his or her submissions, whether orally, in writing or both;
(b) solicit the views of all the parties as to whether the pupil, if he or she is expelled, should be expelled from his or her school only or from all schools of the board; and
(c) solicit the views of all the parties as to whether, if the pupil is not expelled, the board should confirm the suspension originally imposed under section 310, confirm the suspension but reduce its duration or withdraw the suspension.
[S.O. 2007, c. 14, s. 4, in force February 1, 2008]

(6) **Decision** — After completing the hearing, the board shall decide,
(a) whether to expel the pupil; and
(b) if the pupil is to be expelled, whether the pupil is expelled from his or her school only or from all schools of the board.
[S.O. 2007, c. 14, s. 4, in force February 1, 2008]

(7) **Factors board must consider** — In making the decisions required under subsection (6), the board shall take into account,
(a) all submissions and views of the parties, including their views as to whether the pupil, if expelled, should be expelled from his or her school only or from all schools of the board;
(b) any mitigating or other factors prescribed by the regulations; and
(c) any written response to the principal's report recommending expulsion that a person gave to the board under subsection 311.1 (7) before the completion of the hearing.
[S.O. 2007, c. 14, s. 4, in force February 1, 2008]

(8) **Restriction on expulsion** — The board shall not expel a pupil if more than 20 school days have expired since the pupil was suspended under section 310, unless the parties to the expulsion hearing agree on a later deadline.
[S.O. 2007, c. 14, s. 4, in force February 1, 2008]

(9) **Committee** — The board may authorize a committee of at least three members of the board to exercise and perform powers and duties on behalf of the board under this section, and may impose conditions and restrictions on the committee.
[S.O. 2007, c. 14, s. 4, in force February 1, 2008]

311.4 (1) **If pupil not expelled** — If a board does not expel a pupil, the board shall, with respect to the suspension originally imposed under section 310,
(a) confirm the suspension and the duration of the suspension;

(b) confirm the suspension, but shorten its duration, even if the suspension that is under appeal has already been served, and order that the record of the suspension be amended accordingly; or

(c) quash the suspension and order that the record of the suspension be expunged, even if the suspension that is under appeal has already been served.

[S.O. 2007, c. 14, s. 4, in force February 1, 2008]

(2) **Factors board must consider** — In determining which action to take under subsection (1), the board shall take into account,

(a) any submissions made by the parties as to whether the suspension and its duration should be confirmed, the suspension should be confirmed but its duration reduced or the suspension should be withdrawn;

(b) any mitigating or other factors prescribed by the regulations.

[S.O. 2007, c. 14, s. 4, in force February 1, 2008]

(3) **Notice that pupil not expelled** — After determining which action to take under subsection (1), the board shall give written notice containing the following to every person who was entitled to be a party to the expulsion hearing under subsection 311.3 (3):

1. A statement indicating that the pupil is not expelled.
2. A statement indicating whether the board has, under subsection (1), confirmed the suspension and its duration, confirmed the suspension but reduced its duration or withdrawn the suspension.

[S.O. 2007, c. 14, s. 4, in force February 1, 2008]

(4) **Decision final** — The decision of the board under subsection (1) is final.

[S.O. 2007, c. 14, s. 4, in force February 1, 2008]

311.5 If pupil expelled — If a board expels a pupil, the board shall assign the pupil to,

(a) in the case of a pupil expelled from his or her school only, another school of the board; and

(b) in the case of a pupil expelled from all schools of the board, a program for expelled pupils.

[S.O. 2007, c. 14, s. 4, in force February 1, 2008]

311.6 (1) **Notice of expulsion** — A board that expels a pupil shall ensure that written notice of the expulsion is given promptly to,

(a) all the parties to the expulsion hearing; and

(b) the pupil, if the pupil was not a party to the expulsion hearing.

[S.O. 2007, c. 14, s. 4, in force February 1, 2008]

(2) **Contents of notice** — The notice under subsection (1) must include the following:
1. The reason for the expulsion.
2. A statement indicating whether the pupil is expelled from his or her school only or from all schools of the board.
3. Information about the school or program for expelled pupils to which the pupil is assigned.
4. Information about the right to appeal under section 311.7, including the steps that must be taken to appeal.

[S.O. 2007, c. 14, s. 4, in force February 1, 2008]

311.7 (1) **Appeal of expulsion** — In this section, "designated tribunal" means a tribunal designated under the regulations to hear appeals of board decisions to expel pupils.

[S.O. 2007, c. 14, s. 4, in force February 1, 2008]

(2) **Certain persons may appeal** — The following persons may appeal a board's decision to expel a pupil, whether the pupil is expelled from his or her school only or from all schools of the board, to the designated tribunal:
1. The pupil's parent or guardian, unless,
   i. the pupil is at least 18 years old, or
   ii. the pupil is 16 or 17 years old and has withdrawn from parental control.
2. The pupil, if,
   i. the pupil is at least 18 years old, or
   ii. the pupil is 16 or 17 years old and has withdrawn from parental control.
3. Such other persons as may be specified by the designated tribunal.

[S.O. 2007, c. 14, s. 4, in force February 1, 2008]

(3) **Hearing** — The designated tribunal shall hear and determine an appeal under this section, and, for that purpose, it has the powers and duties set out in the regulations.

[S.O. 2007, c. 14, s. 4, in force February 1, 2008]

(4) **Parties to appeal** — The parties to the appeal are:
1. The board.
2. The pupil, if,
   i. the pupil is at least 18 years old, or
   ii. the pupil is 16 or 17 years old and has withdrawn from parental control.
3. The pupil's parent or guardian, if the parent or guardian appealed the decision.

4. The person who appealed the decision to expel the pupil, if the decision was appealed by a person other than the pupil or the pupil's parent or guardian.
[S.O. 2007, c. 14, s. 4, in force February 1, 2008]

(5) **Decision final** — The decision of the designated tribunal on an appeal under this section is final.
[S.O. 2007, c. 14, s. 4, in force February 1, 2008]

(6) **Regulations** — The Minister may make regulations,
(a) designating a tribunal to hear appeals of board decisions to expel pupils;
(b) prescribing the procedures to be followed on an appeal under this section;
(c) prescribing the powers and duties of a designated tribunal under this section.
[S.O. 2007, c. 14, s. 4, in force February 1, 2008]

312. (1) **Programs for suspended, expelled pupils** — Every board shall provide, in accordance with policies and guidelines issued by the Minister, if any,
(a) at least one program for suspended pupils; and
(b) at least one program for expelled pupils.
[S.O. 2007, c. 14, s. 5(1), in force February 1, 2008]

(2) **Policies and guidelines** — The Minister may establish policies and guidelines with respect to programs for suspended and expelled pupils and may,
(a) impose different requirements on the provision of the programs for different circumstances, different locations or different classes of pupils;
(b) set criteria respecting pupils' eligibility to participate in the programs and respecting the criteria to be met for successful completion of the programs;
(c) require boards to offer plans to assist pupils who have successfully completed a program for expelled pupils with their transition back to school and to set criteria respecting those plans; and
(d) authorize boards, subject to such conditions and restrictions as the Minister imposes, to enter into agreements with other boards for the provision of the programs.
[S.O. 2007, c. 14, s. 5(1), in force February 1, 2008]

312. (3) [Repealed S.O. 2007, c. 14, s. 5(1), effective February 1, 2008]

(4) **Programs for expelled pupils** — The Minister may establish one or more programs for expelled pupils to prepare the pupils to return to

school and may require boards to give specified information about the programs to expelled pupils.
[S.O. 2000, c. 12, s. 3, in force September 1, 2000]

(5) **Same** — The Minister may establish policies and guidelines respecting pupils' eligibility to participate in a program established by the Minister under subsection (4) and respecting the criteria to be met for successful completion of the program.
[S.O. 2000, c. 12, s. 3, in force September 1, 2000; S.O. 2007, c. 14, s. 5(2), in force February 1, 2008]

313. (1) **Status of expelled pupil** — An expelled pupil continues to be a pupil of the board that expelled him or her if the pupil attends a program for expelled pupils,
   (a) offered by that board; or
   (b) offered by another board under an agreement between that board and the board that expelled the pupil.
[S.O. 2007, c. 14, s. 6, in force February 1, 2008]

(2) **Same** — An expelled pupil ceases to be a pupil of the board that expelled him or her if,
   (a) the pupil is assigned by that board to a program for expelled pupils and does not attend the program; or
   (b) the pupil registers as a pupil of another board.
[S.O. 2007, c. 14, s. 6, in force February 1, 2008]

314. (1) **Powers of other board** — If a pupil who has been expelled from one board registers as a pupil of another board, the other board may,
   (a) assign the pupil to a school of that board; or
   (b) assign the pupil to a program for expelled pupils, unless the pupil satisfies the requirements of clause 314.1 (1) (a) or (b) as determined by a person who provides a program for expelled pupils.
[S.O. 2007, c. 14, s. 6, in force February 1, 2008]

(2) **Clarification** — If the other board assigns the expelled pupil to a school without knowing that he or she has been expelled by another board, the board may subsequently remove the pupil from the school and assign him or her to a program for expelled pupils, subject to the following conditions:
   1. The board must assign the pupil to a program for expelled pupils promptly on learning that he or she has been expelled from another board.
   2. The board shall not assign the pupil to a program for expelled pupils if the pupil satisfies the requirements of clause 314.1 (1) (a)

or (b) as determined by a person who provides a program for expelled pupils.
[S.O. 2007, c. 14, s. 6, in force February 1, 2008]

314.1 (1) Return to school after expulsion — A pupil who has been expelled from all schools of a board is entitled to be readmitted to a school of the board if the pupil has, since being expelled,
   (a)   successfully completed a program for expelled pupils; or
   (b)   satisfied the objectives required for the successful completion of a program for expelled pupils.
[S.O. 2007, c. 14, s. 6, in force February 1, 2008]

(2) Determination — The determination of whether an expelled pupil satisfies the requirements of clause (1) (a) or (b) is to be made by a person who provides a program for expelled pupils.
[S.O. 2007, c. 14, s. 6, in force February 1, 2008]

(3) Board must readmit pupil — An expelled pupil may apply in writing to a person designated by the board that expelled him or her to be readmitted to a school of that board and, if the pupil satisfies the requirements of clause (1) (a) or (b) as determined by a person who provides a program for expelled pupils, the board shall,
   (a)   readmit the expelled pupil to a school of the board; and
   (b)   promptly inform the pupil in writing of his or her readmittance.
[S.O. 2007, c. 14, s. 6, in force February 1, 2008]

314.2 Clarification: successful completion of program — A pupil who has successfully completed a program for expelled pupils provided by any board or person under this Part has satisfied the requirements of clause 314.1 (1) (a), and no board shall,
   (a)   require the pupil to attend a program for expelled pupils provided by that board before being admitted to a school of the board; or
   (b)   refuse to admit the pupil on the basis that the pupil completed a program for expelled pupils provided by another board or person.
[S.O. 2007, c. 14, s. 6, in force February 1, 2008]

314.3 Return to original school after expulsion — A pupil who has been expelled from one school of a board but not from all schools of the board may apply in writing to a person designated by the board to be re-assigned to the school from which he or she was expelled.
[S.O. 2007, c. 14, s. 6, in force February 1, 2008]

314.4 Clarification: resident pupils — For greater certainty, nothing in this Part requires a board to admit or readmit a pupil who is not otherwise qualified to be a resident pupil of the board.
[S.O. 2007, c. 14, s. 6, in force February 1, 2008]

314.5 Transitional provisions — In this section and in sections 314.6 to 314.10,

"coming into force date" means the day on which the *Education Amendment Act (Progressive Discipline and School Safety), 2007* comes into force; ("date d'effet")

"new Part XIII" means Part XIII as it reads on the coming into force date; ("nouvelle partie XIII")

"old Part XIII" means Part XIII as it read immediately before the coming into force date. ("ancienne partie XIII")
[S.O. 2007, c. 14, s. 6, in force February 1, 2008]

314.6 (1) **Old Part XIII applies** — Old Part XIII continues to apply with respect to,
- (a) suspensions imposed before the coming into force date; and
- (b) limited and full expulsions imposed under old Part XIII before the coming into force date, subject to the exceptions set out in sections 314.8 and 314.9.

[S.O. 2007, c. 14, s. 6, in force February 1, 2008]

(2) **Same – reviews and appeals** — For greater certainty, old Part XIII continues to apply with respect to the review or appeal of a suspension described in clause (1) (a) and with respect to the appeal of an expulsion described in clause (1) (b) and, without limiting the generality of the foregoing,
- (a) in the case of a review or appeal of a suspension,
  - (i) Ontario Regulation 106/01 (Suspension of a Pupil), as it read immediately before the coming into force date, continues to apply with respect to the review or appeal, and
  - (ii) if the review or appeal was required to be conducted in accordance with the requirements established by board policy, the board policy that was in place under old Part XIII continues to apply with respect to the review or appeal; and
- (b) in the case of an appeal of a board decision to expel a pupil under old Part XIII, Ontario Regulation 37/01 (Expulsion of a Pupil), as it read immediately before the coming into force date, continues to apply with respect to the appeal.

[S.O. 2007, c. 14, s. 6, in force February 1, 2008]

(3) **New Part XIII applies** — If a pupil engaged in an activity before the coming into force date that was an infraction for which a suspension or expulsion could be imposed or was required to be imposed under old Part XIII but no action had been commenced in respect of the activity before the coming into force date, the pupil is subject to new Part XIII in respect of the activity.
[S.O. 2007, c. 14, s. 6, in force February 1, 2008]

314.7 Expulsions under old Part XIII — On the coming into force date, every pupil who is still subject to a limited or full expulsion imposed under old Part XIII is deemed to be a pupil of the board from which he or she was expelled.
[S.O. 2007, c. 14, s. 6, in force February 1, 2008]

314.8 (1) **Pupil subject to limited expulsion** — With respect to any pupil of a board who is still subject to a limited expulsion imposed under old Part XIII on the coming into force date, the board shall,
- (a) assign the pupil to a school of the board and offer a plan to assist the pupil with his or her transition back to school; or
- (b) assign the pupil to a program for expelled pupils provided by the board under subsection 312 (1).

[S.O. 2007, c. 14, s. 6, in force February 1, 2008]

(2) **Return to school** — If a pupil is assigned to a program for expelled pupils under subsection (1), the pupil is not entitled to attend school until the date on which he or she would have been entitled to return to school under subsection 309 (14) of old Part XIII, as it read immediately before the coming into force date.
[S.O. 2007, c. 14, s. 6, in force February 1, 2008]

314.9 (1) **Pupil subject to full expulsion** — With respect to a pupil of a board who is still subject to a full expulsion imposed under old Part XIII on the coming into force date, the board shall, on that date, reassign the pupil to a program for expelled pupils provided by the board under subsection 312 (1).
[S.O. 2007, c. 14, s. 6, in force February 1, 2008]

(2) **Return to school** — Every pupil subject to a full expulsion under old Part XIII may return to school in accordance with new Part XIII and, for the purpose, sections 314.1 and 314.2 of new Part XIII apply with necessary modifications.
[S.O. 2007, c. 14, s. 6, in force February 1, 2008]

314.10 (1) **Regulations – transitional** — The Lieutenant Governor in Council may make regulations providing for any transitional matters that the Lieutenant Governor in Council considers necessary or advisable,
- (a) for the effective implementation of new Part XIII or regulations made under it;
- (b) to facilitate the transition from old Part XIII or regulations made under it to new Part XIII or regulations made under it.

[S.O. 2007, c. 14, s. 6, in force February 1, 2008]

(2) **Scope** — A regulation under this section may be general or particular in its application.

[S.O. 2007, c. 14, s. 6, in force February 1, 2008]

315. (1) **Personal information** — The Minister may collect and may by regulation require boards to collect such personal information as is specified by regulation from, or about, the classes of persons specified by regulation for the following purposes, and the Minister may specify or restrict the manner in which the information is to be collected:
1. To ensure the safety of pupils.
2. To administer programs, courses and services to pupils who are suspended or expelled and to determine whether an expelled pupil has successfully completed a program, course or service and as a result is eligible to return to school.

(2) **Same** — A board or other person is authorized to disclose the personal information collected under subsection (1) to the Minister for the purposes described in that subsection, and the Minister may disclose it to such persons or entities as may be prescribed by regulation for those purposes.

(3) **Definition** — In this section,
"personal information" has the same meaning as in section 38 of the *Freedom of Information and Protection of Privacy Act* and section 28 of the *Municipal Freedom of Information and Protection of Privacy Act*.

316. (1) **Regulations** — The Minister may make regulations,
- (a) prescribing such matters as are required, or permitted, under this Part to be prescribed or to be done by regulation;
- (b) specifying when, during a school day, a suspension of a pupil is permitted to begin and to end.

(2) **Classes** — A regulation under subsection (1) may impose different requirements on different classes of person, place or thing or in different circumstances.

(3) **Exceptions** — A regulation under subsection (1) may provide that one or more provisions of this Part or of the regulation does not apply to specified persons or in specified circumstances.
[S.O. 2000, c. 12, s. 3, in force September 1, 2000]

[**Note:** Sections 317 to 326 repealed S.O. 1997, c. 31, s. 129, in force January 1, 1998]

EDUCATION ACT

R.S.O. 1990, c. E.2

Amendments to s. 265: S.O. 1991, c. 10, s. 6; S.O. 2001, c. 14, Sched. A, s. 8, in force July 1, 2001.

Part X
Teachers, Pupil Records and Education Numbers Duties

Section 265

265. (1) **Duties of principal** — It is the duty of a principal of a school, in addition to the principal's duties as a teacher,

(a) **discipline** — to maintain proper order and discipline in the school;

(b) **co-operation** — to develop co-operation and co-ordination of effort among the members of the staff of the school;

(c) **register pupils and record attendance** — to register the pupils and to ensure that the attendance of pupils for every school day is recorded either in the register supplied by the Minister in accordance with the instructions contained therein or in such other manner as is approved by the Minister;

(d) **pupil records** — in accordance with this Act, the regulations and the guidelines issued by the Minister, to collect information for inclusion in a record in respect of each pupil enrolled in the school and to establish, maintain, retain, transfer and dispose of the record;

(e) **timetable** — to prepare a timetable, to conduct the school according to such timetable and the school year calendar or calendars applicable thereto, to make the calendar or calendars and the timetable accessible to the pupils, teachers and supervisory officers and to assign classes and subjects to the teachers;

(f) **examinations and reports** — to hold, subject to the approval of the appropriate supervisory officer, such examinations as the principal considers necessary for the promotion of pupils or for any other purpose and report as required by the board the progress of the pupil to his or her parent or guardian where the pupil is a minor and otherwise to the pupil;

(g) **promote pupils** — subject to revision by the appropriate supervisory officer, to promote such pupils as the principal considers proper and to issue to each such pupil a statement thereof;

(h) **textbooks** — to ensure that all textbooks used by pupils are those approved by the board and, in the case of subject areas for which the Minister approves textbooks, those approved by the Minister;

(i) **reports** — to furnish to the Ministry and to the appropriate supervisory officer any information that it may be in the principal's power to give respecting the condition of the school premises, the discipline of the school, the progress of the pupils and any other matter affecting the interests of the school, and to prepare such reports for the board as are required by the board;

(j) **care of pupils and property** — to give assiduous attention to the health and comfort of the pupils, to the cleanliness, temperature and ventilation of the school, to the care of all teaching materials and other school property, and to the condition and appearance of the school buildings and grounds;

(k) **report to M.O.H.** — to report promptly to the board and to the medical officer of health when the principal has reason to suspect the existence of any communicable disease in the school, and of the unsanitary condition of any part of the school building or the school grounds;

(l) **persons with communicable diseases** — to refuse admission to the school of any person who the principal believes is infected with or exposed to communicable diseases requiring an order under section 22 of the *Health Protection and Promotion Act* until furnished with a certificate of a medical officer of health or of a legally qualified medical practitioner approved by the medical officer of health that all danger from exposure to contact with such person has passed;

(m) **access to school or class** — subject to an appeal to the board, to refuse to admit to the school or classroom a person whose presence in the school or classroom would in the principal's judgment be detrimental to the physical or mental well-being of the pupils; and

(n) **visitor's book** — to maintain a visitor's book in the school when so determined by the board.

[R.S.O. 1990, c. E.2, s. 265; S.O. 1991, c. 10, s. 6, effective July 1, 2001]

(2) **Co-instructional activities** — In addition, it is the duty of a principal, in accordance with the board plan to provide for co-instructional activities under subsection 170 (1), to develop and implement a school plan providing for co-instructional activities.

[S.O. 2001, c. 14, Sched. A, s. 8, in force July 1, 2001]

(3) **School council** — The principal shall consult the school council at least once in each school year respecting the school plan providing for co-instructional activities.
[S.O. 2001, c. 14, Sched. A, s. 8, in force July 1, 2001]

[Section 265 (4) repealed 2001, c. 14, Sched. A, s. 8, in force July 1, 2001]

ACCESS TO SCHOOL PREMISES

O. Reg. 474/00

Amendments to ss. 2-4: O. Reg. 471/07, in force February 1, 2008.

1. This Regulation governs access to school premises under section 305 of the Act.

2. (1) Subject to any restrictions set out in this regulation, the following persons are permitted to be on school premises when the premises are being used for a purpose authorized by the board:
[O. Reg. 471/07, s. 1, in force February 1, 2008]

1. A person enrolled as a pupil in the school.
2. A parent or guardian of such a pupil.
3. A person employed or retained by the board.
4. A person who is otherwise on the premises for a lawful purpose.

(2) A person who is invited to attend an event, a class or a meeting on school premises is permitted to be on the premises for that purpose.

(3) A person who is invited onto school premises for a particular purpose by the principal, a vice-principal or another person authorized by board policy to do so is permitted to be on the premises for that purpose.

(4) Subsection (1), (2) or (3) does not entitle a person to have access to all areas of the school premises.

(5) Subsection (1) does not restrict the right of the board to lock the school premises when the premises are not being used for a purpose authorized by the board.

3. (1) A person is not permitted to remain on school premises if his or her presence is detrimental to the safety or well-being of a person on the premises, in the judgment of the principal, a vice-principal or another person authorized by the board to make such a determination.

(2) A person is not permitted to remain on school premises if a policy of the board requires the person to report his or her presence on the premises in a specified manner and the person fails to do so.

(3) Subsections (1) and (2) do not apply to a pupil enrolled in the school or to a pupil attending a program for suspended or expelled pupils that is located on the school premises.
[O. Reg. 471/07, s. 2, in force February 1, 2008]

4. A person who is not permitted, under section 3, to be on or remain on school premises on January 31, 2008, shall be permitted to be on and remain on school premises in accordance with this regulation on and after February 1, 2008, if the person was a pupil enrolled in the school at the time that permission for him or her to be on or remain on school premises was revoked.

[O. Reg. 471/07, s. 3, in force February 1, 2008]

SUSPENSION AND EXPULSION OF PUPILS

O. Reg. 472/07

[in force February 1, 2008]

No amendments.

1. Definition — In this Regulation, "designated tribunal" means the Child and Family Services Review Board continued under section 207 of the *Child and Family Services Act*.

[O. Reg. 472/07, s. 1, in force February 1, 2008]

2. Mitigating factors — For the purposes of subsections 306 (2), 306 (4), 310 (3), 311.1 (4) and clauses 311.3 (7) (b) and 311.4 (2) (b) of the Act, the following mitigating factors shall be taken into account:

1. The pupil does not have the ability to control his or her behaviour.
2. The pupil does not have the ability to understand the foreseeable consequences of his or her behaviour.
3. The pupil's continuing presence in the school does not create an unacceptable risk to the safety of any person.

[O. Reg. 472/07, s. 2, in force February 1, 2008]

3. Other factors — For the purposes of subsections 306 (2), 306 (4), 310 (3), 311.1 (4) and clauses 311.3 (7) (b) and 311.4 (2) (b) of the Act, the following other factors shall be taken into account if they would mitigate the seriousness of the activity for which the pupil may be or is being suspended or expelled:

1. The pupil's history.
2. Whether a progressive discipline approach has been used with the pupil.
3. Whether the activity for which the pupil may be or is being suspended or expelled was related to any harassment of the pupil because of his or her race, ethnic origin, religion, disability, gender or sexual orientation or to any other harassment.
4. How the suspension or expulsion would affect the pupil's ongoing education.
5. The age of the pupil.

6. In the case of a pupil for whom an individual education plan has been developed,
    i. whether the behaviour was a manifestation of a disability identified in the pupil's individual education plan,
    ii. whether appropriate individualized accommodation has been provided, and
    iii. whether the suspension or expulsion is likely to result in an aggravation or worsening of the pupil's behaviour or conduct.
[O. Reg. 472/07, s. 3, in force February 1, 2008]

4. Child and Family Services Review Board — The Child and Family Services Review Board is designated for the purposes of the definition of "designated tribunal" in subsection 311.7 (1) of the Act to hear appeals of board decisions to expel pupils.
[O. Reg. 472/07, s. 4, in force February 1, 2008]

5. (1) **Notice of appeal** — To appeal a board's decision to expel a pupil, a person who is entitled, under subsection 311.7 (2) of the Act, to appeal the decision shall give the designated tribunal a written notice of appeal within 30 days after the date on which he or she is considered, in accordance with the rules set out in subsection 300 (3) of the Act, to have received the notice given under subsection 311.6 (1) of the Act.
[O. Reg. 472/07, s. 5(1), in force February 1, 2008]

(2) The designated tribunal may extend the period of time for giving the written notice of appeal, before or after the expiry of the period, if it is satisfied that there are reasonable grounds for the extension.
[O. Reg. 472/07, s. 5(2), in force February 1, 2008]

(3) The notice of appeal shall,
(a) set out the date of the decision that is being appealed;
(b) set out the name of the board that made the decision;
(c) state whether the decision expels the pupil from his or her school only or from all schools of the board; and
(d) be in a form acceptable to the designated tribunal.
[O. Reg. 472/07, s. 5(3), in force February 1, 2008]

(4) The designated tribunal shall not refuse to deal with an appeal on the ground that there is a deficiency in the content or form of the notice of appeal.
[O. Reg. 472/07, s. 5(4), in force February 1, 2008]

6. (1) **Hearing of appeal** — The designated tribunal shall commence a hearing within 30 days after receiving a written notice of appeal.
[O. Reg. 472/07, s. 6(1), in force February 1, 2008]

(2) The designated tribunal may extend the period of time for commencing the hearing, before or after the expiry of the period, at the request of any party to the appeal.
[O. Reg. 472/07, s. 6(2), in force February 1, 2008]

(3) A pupil whose expulsion is being appealed has the right to be present at the hearing and to make a statement on his or her own behalf, whether or not the pupil is a party to the appeal.
[O. Reg. 472/07, s. 6(3), in force February 1, 2008]

(4) After hearing an appeal from a decision of a board, the designated tribunal shall do one of the following:
1. Confirm the board's decision to expel the pupil.
2. If the board's decision was to expel the pupil from his or her school only, quash the expulsion and reinstate the pupil to the school.
3. If the board's decision was to expel the pupil from all schools of the board,
    i. change the expulsion to an expulsion from the pupil's school only, or
    ii. quash the expulsion and reinstate the pupil to his or her school.

[O. Reg. 472/07, s. 6(4), in force February 1, 2008]

(5) The designated tribunal shall provide each party, or the party's counsel or agent, with,
(a) its decision on the appeal within 10 days after completing the hearing; and
(b) written reasons for its decision within 30 days after completing the hearing.

[O. Reg. 472/07, s. 6(5), in force February 1, 2008]

(6) If the designated tribunal changes an expulsion from all schools of the board to an expulsion from the pupil's school only or quashes an expulsion and reinstates the pupil to his or her school, it may order that any record of the expulsion of the pupil be expunged or amended if the designated tribunal considers it appropriate in the circumstances.
[O. Reg. 472/07, s. 6(6), in force February 1, 2008]

7. [O. Reg. 472/07, s. 6(7), in force February 1, 2008] OMITTED (REVOKES OTHER REGULATIONS).

8. [O. Reg. 472/07, s. 6(8), in force February 1, 2008] OMITTED (PROVIDES FOR COMING INTO FORCE OF PROVISIONS OF THIS REGULATION).

APPENDIX

APPENDIX A

Policy/Program Memorandum No. 128

Date of Issue: October 4, 2007   **Effective:** Until revoked or modified

Subject: THE PROVINCIAL CODE OF CONDUCT AND SCHOOL BOARD CODES OF CONDUCT

Application: Directors of Education
Superintendents of School Authorities
Principals of Elementary Schools
Principals of Secondary Schools
Principals of Provincial Schools
Chairs of Special Education Advisory Committees

Reference: This memorandum replaces Policy/Program Memorandum No. 128, November 14, 2000.

INTRODUCTION

The provincial Code of Conduct has been revised to reflect changes made in the Education Act that pertain to suspension and expulsion of students. On June 4, 2007, the Education Amendment Act (Progressive Discipline and School Safety), 2007, was passed, amending Part XIII of the Education Act dealing with behaviour, discipline, and safety. These amendments come into force February 1, 2008.

The revised provincial Code of Conduct is communicated in this memorandum.[1]

This memorandum also gives direction to school boards[2] on reviewing their own codes of conduct and the local codes of conduct in their schools. Boards must review their codes of conduct to ensure that they are consistent with the provincial Code of Conduct, and must have necessary revisions in place by February 1, 2008.

Boards should note that subsection 301(2) of Part XIII of the Education Act, which outlines the purposes of the provincial Code of Conduct, remains unchanged. The rest of section 301, which relates to the Minister's powers, and all of section 302, which authorizes school board policies, also remain largely unchanged.

For excerpts from the relevant sections of the legislation, see the Appendix to this memorandum.

A school should be a place that promotes responsibility, respect, civility, and academic excellence in a safe learning and teaching environment. A positive school climate exists when all members of the school community feel safe, comfortable, and accepted.

All students,[3] parents,[4] teachers, and staff members have the right to be safe, and to feel safe, in their school community. With this right comes the responsibility to contribute to a positive school climate. The promotion of strategies and initiatives such as Student Success and character development, along with the employment of prevention and intervention strategies to address inappropriate behaviour, fosters a positive school climate that supports academic achievement for all students. Boards and schools should therefore focus on prevention and early intervention as the key to maintaining a positive school environment in which students can learn and teachers can teach.

Policy/Program Memorandum No. 145, "Progressive Discipline and Promoting Positive Student Behaviour", October 4, 2007, provides an overview of the progressive discipline approach to be used when addressing issues of student conduct. When inappropriate behaviour occurs, Ontario schools will be required to utilize a range of interventions, supports, and consequences that are developmentally appropriate, that include opportunities for students to learn from mistakes, and that focus on improving behaviour. In some circumstances, short-term suspension may be a useful tool. In the case of a serious incident, long-term suspension or expulsion, which is further along the continuum of progressive discipline, may be the response that is required.

The provincial Code of Conduct sets clear provincial standards of behaviour. These standards of behaviour apply not only to students, but also to all individuals involved in the publicly funded school system – parents, volunteers, teachers, and other staff members – whether they are on school property, on school buses, at school-related events or activities, or in other circumstances that could have an impact on the school climate.

Responsible citizenship involves appropriate participation in the civic life of the school community. Active and engaged citizens are aware of their rights, but more importantly, they accept responsibility for protecting their rights and the rights of others.

Requirements for School Boards

Boards are required to:

> revise their board code of conduct and, if applicable, require principals[5] to engage in reviews of school codes of conduct to incorporate changes in the provincial Code of Conduct, as outlined in this memorandum;
>
> inform staff members, students, parents, and the school community of the terms of the revised provincial Code of Conduct and school board codes of conduct.

Revision of School Board Codes of Conduct

The standards of behaviour in school board codes of conduct must be consistent with the requirements set out in this memorandum. In reviewing their codes of conduct, school boards must consult with school councils. They should also consult with a wide variety of stakeholders, including parents, principals, teachers, students, their Parent Involvement Committee, their Special Education Advisory Committee, community partners, community agencies,[6] members of Aboriginal communities (e.g., Elders), and those groups that are traditionally not consulted. School board codes of conduct must:

> include the standards stated in the provincial Code of Conduct;
>
> set out standards of behaviour for all members of the school community (e.g., parents, students, staff, visitors, volunteers);
>
> link locally developed standards to the relevant provincial standards (e.g., school board rules for the use of electronic devices such as cellphones could be linked to the provincial standard requiring those at school to "respect the need of others to work in an environment that is conducive to learning and teaching" [see Respect, Civility, and Responsible Citizenship]);
>
> indicate where and/or when these standards will apply (e.g., in school sports activities, on school buses, in off-site school-sponsored activities, or in circumstances where engaging in an activity could have a negative impact on the school climate);

include procedures and timelines for review (reviews must be conducted at least every three years).

Development or Revision of Local Codes of Conduct in Schools

School boards may continue to require principals to develop additional codes of conduct tailored expressly for their schools. Where local codes have been developed, they must be reviewed to ensure that they are consistent with the provincial Code of Conduct and other requirements in this memorandum. These codes must set out clearly what is acceptable and what is unacceptable behaviour for all members of the elementary or secondary school community (e.g., parents, students, staff, visitors, volunteers), and must also be consistent with the school board's code of conduct.

In developing or reviewing these local standards of behaviour, the principal must take into consideration the views of the school council. In addition, he or she should:

- seek input from students, staff, parents, and members of the school community;
- include procedures and timelines for review, in accordance with school board policy;
- develop a communications plan that outlines how these standards will be made clear to everyone, including parents whose first language is a language other than English or French.

School boards should assist principals in developing or reviewing their local codes of conduct by creating clear guidelines for the development of such codes, in keeping with provincial policy.

These local codes of conduct should also be communicated to all members of the school community.

The Provincial Code of Conduct

Purposes of the Code

Subsection 301(1) of Part XIII of the Education Act states that "the Minister may establish a code of conduct governing the behaviour of all persons in schools". Subsection 301(2) sets out the purposes of this provincial code of conduct, as follows:

1. To ensure that all members of the school community, especially people in positions of authority, are treated with respect and dignity.
2. To promote responsible citizenship by encouraging appropriate participation in the civic life of the school community.
3. To maintain an environment where conflict and difference can be addressed in a manner characterized by respect and civility.
4. To encourage the use of non-violent means to resolve conflict.
5. To promote the safety of people in the schools.
6. To discourage the use of alcohol and illegal drugs.

Standards of Behaviour

Respect, Civility, and Responsible Citizenship

All members of the school community must:

> respect and comply with all applicable federal, provincial, and municipal laws;
>
> demonstrate honesty and integrity;
>
> respect differences in people, their ideas, and their opinions;
>
> treat one another with dignity and respect at all times, and especially when there is disagreement;
>
> respect and treat others fairly, regardless of, for example, race, ancestry, place of origin, colour, ethnic origin, citizenship, religion, gender, sexual orientation, age, or disability;
>
> respect the rights of others;
>
> show proper care and regard for school property and the property of others;
>
> take appropriate measures to help those in need;
>
> seek assistance from a member of the school staff, if necessary, to resolve conflict peacefully;
>
> respect all members of the school community, especially persons in positions of authority;

respect the need of others to work in an environment that is conducive to learning and teaching;

not swear at a teacher or at another person in a position of authority.

Safety

All members of the school community must not:

engage in bullying behaviours;

commit sexual assault;

traffic weapons or illegal drugs;

give alcohol to a minor;

commit robbery;

be in possession of any weapon, including firearms;

use any object to threaten or intimidate another person;

cause injury to any person with an object;

be in possession of, or be under the influence of, or provide others with alcohol or illegal drugs;

inflict or encourage others to inflict bodily harm on another person;

engage in hate propaganda and other forms of behaviour motivated by hate or bias;

commit an act of vandalism that causes extensive damage to school property or to property located on the premises of the school.

Roles and Responsibilities

School Boards

School boards provide direction to their schools to ensure opportunity, academic excellence, and accountability in the education system. It is the responsibility of school boards to:

develop policies that set out how their schools will implement and enforce the provincial Code of Conduct and all other rules that they develop that are related to the provincial standards that promote and support respect, civility, responsible citizenship, and safety;

review these policies regularly with students, staff, parents, volunteers, and the community;

seek input from school councils, their Parent Involvement Committee, their Special Education Advisory Committee, parents, students, staff members, and the school community;

establish a process that clearly communicates the provincial Code of Conduct and school board codes of conduct to all parents, students, staff members, and members of the school community in order to obtain their commitment and support;

develop effective intervention strategies and respond to all infractions related to the standards for respect, civility, responsible citizenship, and safety;

provide opportunities for all of the staff to acquire the knowledge, skills, and attitudes necessary to develop and maintain academic excellence in a safe learning and teaching environment.

Wherever possible, boards should collaborate to provide coordinated prevention and intervention programs and services, and should endeavour to share effective practices.

Principals

Under the direction of their school boards, principals take a leadership role in the daily operation of a school. They provide this leadership by:

demonstrating care for the school community and a commitment to academic excellence in a safe teaching and learning environment;

holding everyone under their authority accountable for his or her behaviour and actions;

empowering students to be positive leaders in their school and community;

communicating regularly and meaningfully with all members of their school community.

Teachers and Other School Staff Members

Under the leadership of their principals, teachers and other school staff members maintain order in the school and are expected to hold everyone to the highest standard of respectful and responsible behaviour. As role models, teachers and school staff uphold these high standards when they:

> help students work to their full potential and develop their sense of self-worth;
>
> empower students to be positive leaders in their classroom, school, and community;
>
> communicate regularly and meaningfully with parents;
>
> maintain consistent standards of behaviour for all students;
>
> demonstrate respect for all students, staff, parents, volunteers, and the members of the school community;
>
> prepare students for the full responsibilities of citizenship.

Students

Students are to be treated with respect and dignity. In return, they must demonstrate respect for themselves, for others, and for the responsibilities of citizenship through acceptable behaviour. Respect and responsibility are demonstrated when a student:

> comes to school prepared, on time, and ready to learn;
>
> shows respect for himself or herself, for others, and for those in authority;
>
> refrains from bringing anything to school that may compromise the safety of others;
>
> follows the established rules and takes responsibility for his or her own actions.

Parents

Parents play an important role in the education of their children, and can support the efforts of school staff in maintaining a safe and respectful learning environment for all students. Parents fulfil their role when they:

> show an active interest in their child's school work and progress;
>
> communicate regularly with the school;
>
> help their child be neat, appropriately dressed, and prepared for school;
>
> ensure that their child attends school regularly and on time;
>
> promptly report to the school their child's absence or late arrival;
>
> show that they are familiar with the provincial Code of Conduct, the board's code of conduct, and school rules;
>
> encourage and assist their child in following the rules of behaviour;
>
> assist school staff in dealing with disciplinary issues involving their child.

Community Partners and the Police

Through outreach, partnerships already in place may be enhanced and new partnerships with community agencies and members of the community (e.g., Aboriginal Elders) may also be created. Community agencies are resources that boards can use to deliver prevention or intervention programs. Protocols are effective ways of establishing linkages between boards and community agencies and of formalizing the relationship between them. These partnerships must respect all applicable collective agreements.

The police play an essential role in making our schools and communities safer. The police investigate incidents in accordance with the protocol developed with the local school board. These protocols are based on a provincial model that was developed by the Ministry of the Solicitor General and the Ministry of Education.

Appendix: Excerpts From the Legislation

Education Act

Part XIII contains the following requirements that apply to school boards and schools:

> Every board shall take such steps as the Minister directs to bring the code of conduct to the attention of pupils, parents and guardians of pupils and others who may be present in schools under the jurisdiction of the board. s. 301(3)
>
> Every board shall establish policies and guidelines with respect to the conduct of persons in schools within the board's jurisdiction and the policies and guidelines must address such matters and include such requirements as the Minister may specify. s. 302(1)
>
> When establishing policies and guidelines under [section 302], a board shall consider the views of school councils with respect to the contents of the policies and guidelines. s. 302(8)
>
> The board shall periodically review its policies and guidelines established under [section 302] and shall solicit the views of pupils, teachers, staff, volunteers working in the schools, parents and guardians, school councils and the public. s. 302(9)
>
> A board may direct the principal of a school to establish a local code of conduct governing the behaviour of all persons in the school, and the local code must be consistent with the provincial code established under subsection 301(1) and must address such matters and include such requirements as the board may specify. s. 303(1)
>
> A board shall direct a principal to establish a local code of conduct if the board is required to do so by the Minister, and the local code must address such matters and include such requirements as the Minister may specify. s. 303(2)
>
> When establishing or reviewing a local code of conduct, the principal shall consider the views of the school council with respect to its contents. s. 303(3)

Education Act, as amended by the Education Amendment Act (Progressive Discipline and School Safety), 2007

Relevant excerpts from the sections of the Education Act, as amended by the Education Amendment Act (Progressive Discipline and School Safety), 2007, are provided below for reference.

Suspension

Activities leading to possible suspension

306. (1) A principal shall consider whether to suspend a pupil if he or she believes that the pupil has engaged in any of the following activities while at school, at a school-related activity or in other circumstances where engaging in the activity will have an impact on the school climate:

1. Uttering a threat to inflict serious bodily harm on another person.
2. Possessing alcohol or illegal drugs.
3. Being under the influence of alcohol.
4. Swearing at a teacher or at another person in a position of authority.
5. Committing an act of vandalism that causes extensive damage to school property at the pupil's school or to property located on the premises of the pupil's school.
6. Bullying.
7. Any other activity that is an activity for which a principal may suspend a pupil under a policy of the board.

Suspension, Investigation and Possible Expulsion

Activities leading to suspension

310. (1) A principal shall suspend a pupil if he or she believes that the pupil has engaged in any of the following activities while at school, at a school-related activity or in other circumstances where engaging in the activity will have an impact on the school climate:

1. Possessing a weapon, including possessing a firearm.
2. Using a weapon to cause or to threaten bodily harm to another person.

3. Committing physical assault on another person that causes bodily harm requiring treatment by a medical practitioner.

4. Committing sexual assault.

5. Trafficking in weapons or in illegal drugs.

6. Committing robbery.

7. Giving alcohol to a minor.

8. Any other activity that, under a policy of a board, is an activity for which a principal must suspend a pupil and, therefore in accordance with this Part, conduct an investigation to determine whether to recommend to the board that the pupil be expelled.

---

[1] *Ontario Schools – Code of Conduct*, a booklet published by the Ministry of Education in 2000, is superseded by the Code of Conduct communicated in this memorandum.

[2] In this memorandum, *school board(s)* and *board(s)* refer to district school boards and school authorities.

[3] The term *student*, as used in this memorandum, refers to *pupil*, as used in the *Education Act*.

[4] In this memorandum, *parent(s)* refers to parent(s) and guardian(s). Parental involvement applies, except in cases where the student is eighteen years of age or over or is sixteen or seventeen years of age and has "withdrawn from parental control".

[5] In this memorandum, *principal* refers to the principal or to a person designated by the principal or by the board.

[6] Community agencies include a range of community service agencies, local organizations, and programs.

APPENDIX B

Policy/Program Memorandum No. 141

Date of Issue:	August 23, 2007 **Effective:** Until revoked or modified
Subject:	**SCHOOL BOARD PROGRAMS FOR STUDENTS ON LONG-TERM SUSPENSION**
Application:	Directors of Education Superintendents of School Authorities Principals of Elementary Schools Principals of Secondary Schools Principals of Provincial Schools Special Education Advisory Committees
References:	The Education Act, as amended by the Education Amendment Act (Progressive Discipline and School Safety), 2007. Ontario Regulation 472/07, "Suspension and Expulsion of Pupils". Policy/Program Memorandum No. 142, "School Board Programs for Expelled Students", August 23, 2007.

Introduction

The Ministry of Education is committed to ensuring that all students[1] who are on long-term suspension have the opportunity to continue their education. The Education Act, as amended by the Education Amendment Act (Progressive Discipline and School Safety), 2007, requires school boards[2] to offer at least one board program for suspended students as of February 1, 2008. In this document, *long-term suspension* means a suspension of more than five school days.

The purpose of this memorandum is to provide direction to school boards regarding the development of board programs for students on long-term suspension. For excerpts from the relevant sections of the Education Act and the regulation, see the Appendix to this memorandum.

With respect to programs for students on long-term suspension, research[3] has demonstrated that positive outcomes for students are related to specific program elements that are tailored to meet the needs of each student. The active engagement of parents[4] and families and linkages to community agencies,[5] such as agencies that provide counselling support, also contribute to positive overall outcomes for students.

In the case of students with special education needs, boards are required to provide appropriate support consistent with the student's Individual Education Plan (IEP).

It is expected that boards will actively encourage suspended students to participate in the board program for suspended students. However, boards cannot compel students on long-term suspension to participate in a board program for suspended students.

Resources that are dedicated to programs for students on long-term suspension may also be used to benefit students who have not been suspended but who have shown behaviours that, if unchanged, could lead to a suspension. However, the needs of students on long-term suspension remain the priority.

General Requirements

As stated above, boards must offer at least one program for students who are on long-term suspension. In the written notice of suspension, parents must be notified of the board program to which the student on long-term suspension has been assigned.

While boards are not required to provide programs for students who have been suspended for less than six days, boards are expected to provide homework packages for these students to help ensure that they do not fall behind in their school work.

Considerations for Program Development

In developing programs, boards have the flexibility to take into account local needs and circumstances, such as geographical considerations, demographics, cultural needs, and availability of board and community supports and resources.

Boards should draw upon evidence-based practices that promote positive student behaviour. For example, the program should incorporate board-wide initiatives such as character development and bullying prevention.

In the development of board policies related to the creation of these programs, boards should consult with parents, principals,[6] teachers, students, school councils, their Parent Involvement Committee, their Special Education Advisory Committee, community partners, social service agencies, members of Aboriginal communities (e.g., Elders), and those groups that are traditionally not consulted.

Boards must take into account the needs of individual students by showing sensitivity to diversity and to cultural needs in their programs for students on long-term suspension. Their programs should be in keeping with the relevant ministry policies on antiracism and ethnocultural equity and antidiscrimination education and with the principles in the ministry document *Ontario First Nation, Métis, and Inuit Education Policy Framework, 2007*.

Boards are required to adhere to the Municipal Freedom of Information and Protection of Privacy Act, the Ontario Human Rights Code, and the Education Act and regulations made under the Act in the development and implementation of programs. Boards should consult with their legal counsel and freedom of information coordinators to ensure that they are fulfilling their legal responsibilities.

School Board Policies on Program Operation

School boards are required to develop policies regarding the operation of their programs for students who are suspended. These policies must deal with, but not be limited to, the following issues:

> discipline (e.g., what constitutes unacceptable behaviour and the consequences of such behaviour)
>
> safety (e.g., what measures will be taken to ensure a safe learning and teaching environment)

Boards are expected to make their policies publicly available. Boards are also expected to provide their policies directly to students and their parents before and/or upon entry to a program for suspended students. In particular, students and their parents must be informed of the discipline and safety rules and the ways in which the rules will be implemented. Boards are advised to consult their legal counsel in the development of these policies, particularly on the aspects related to discipline and safety.

Program Requirements

A Student Action Plan (SAP) must be developed for every student on a long-term suspension who makes a commitment to attend the board program for suspended students.

Programs for Students on a Suspension of Six to Ten School Days

The program provided for in the SAP must include an academic component to support the student on a long-term suspension of six to ten school days in continuing his or her education. Boards are not required to provide a non-academic component for suspensions of this length. However, boards should consider what types of support, if any, the student may require during the suspension and upon his or her return to school. The board must also consider continuing any supports that may have been in place for the student prior to the suspension. In the case of students with special education needs, boards are required to provide appropriate support consistent with the student's IEP.

Programs for Students on a Suspension of Eleven to Twenty School Days

The program provided for in the SAP will consist of both an academic and a non-academic component to support the student on a long-term suspension of eleven to twenty school days in continuing his or her education. The board must also consider continuing any types of support that may have been in place for the student prior to the suspension. In the case of students with special education needs, boards are required to provide appropriate support consistent with the student's IEP.

If a student on a long-term suspension pending an expulsion hearing is expelled, and the student makes a commitment to attend a board program for expelled students, the SAP should be carried forward into the new program.

Components of Programs for Students on Long-Term Suspension

Boards are responsible for determining the content and balance of the program for each student for both the academic and non-academic components of the program. The content and balance of the program for a student will depend on the needs of the student, the length of the suspension, and the nature and severity of the behaviour that led to the suspension, including any mitigating or other factors.

Academic Component

The purpose of the academic component is to ensure that all students on a long-term suspension (more than five school days) have the opportunity to continue their education. Boards must provide students with the opportunity to continue or complete programs of study, including assignments, homework, and any other work evaluated in their regular classes. In all cases, every effort must be made to maintain the student's regular academic course work throughout the suspension period.

The academic component must follow the curriculum outlined in the Ontario curriculum policy documents, unless the student has an IEP that provides for modifications to the Ontario curriculum or an alternative program. The academic component may include, but is not limited to, the provision of distance learning, e-learning, remedial help in literacy and numeracy, individual instruction, and/or opportunities within the board.

Elementary school students must be supported in continuing to acquire the necessary knowledge and skills outlined in the Ontario curriculum policy documents for elementary schools.

Secondary school students must be supported in continuing to earn credits towards their Ontario Secondary School Diploma.

Non-academic Component

The purpose of the non-academic component is to assist students on a long-term suspension of more than ten school days in the development of positive attitudes and behaviours. Identifying and addressing the underlying causes of the student's behaviour will help reduce the risk that the student might be given a suspension or expulsion in the future.

For those students on a suspension of six to ten school days, boards should consider what types of support, if any, the student may require during the suspension and upon his or her return to school.

Students may require a range of services and types of support that may include access to culturally appropriate support. The board should make appropriate support available and/or facilitate a student's referral to community agencies and/or provide support through other methods, such as remote access to resources (e.g., video conferencing, telepsychiatry). To meet the alternative programming requirements of a student with special education needs, the board should refer to the student's IEP.

Protocols between boards and community agencies should be in place to facilitate referral processes and the provision of services and support for students and their parents and families. Where such protocols already exist, they should be reviewed, and where they do not, new protocols should be developed to increase the board's capacity to respond to the needs of students on long-term suspension.

Developing and Implementing the Student Action Plan

An SAP must be developed for every student on long-term suspension who makes a commitment to attend the board program. The SAP will outline the objectives for students and be tailored to meet the specific needs of the student.

The student and/or his or her parent(s) must notify the principal verbally or in writing that the student is committed to attending the program. Once the principal has received this notification, development of the SAP must begin immediately. The SAP must be implemented as soon as possible. It is expected that the SAP, with appropriate support, will facilitate the continuation of the student's learning during the suspension period. Every effort must be made to provide an opportunity for the student to maintain his or her regular academic course work throughout the suspension period.

The SAP will be developed by the principal in cooperation with appropriate staff, the student, and his or her parent(s). It is important that parents participate in the development and implementation of the SAP on an ongoing basis. Boards should make reasonable efforts to enable parents to participate by, for example, reaching out to community members who can provide translation services for those whose first language is not English or French.

It is the responsibility of the board to coordinate the types of support required to assist the student in continuing his or her learning. For students with special education needs, boards are required to provide appropriate support consistent with the student's IEP.

For students on a long-term suspension pending expulsion, boards are also expected to provide a homework package until the SAP is in place. As stated earlier, in the case of an expelled student who attended a program for students on long-term suspension, the student's SAP should be carried forward into the program for expelled students.

The Planning Meeting

Once the student and/or his or her parent(s) have indicated that the student is committed to attending the program, the principal shall hold a planning meeting. The planning meeting should be a collaborative process and must include school and board staff and the student. Where possible, the student's parent(s) or other significant family member(s), as well as the student's teacher(s), should also be present at the meeting. Principals should make reasonable efforts to include parents in this meeting. If the parents cannot be present, the planning meeting should proceed nevertheless, and the principal must attempt to follow up with the parent(s) of the student as soon after the meeting as possible. In addition, where appropriate, community agency staff and any other relevant persons or professionals should also be included in the planning meeting.

The purpose of the planning meeting is to:

> identify the needs of the student;
>
> identify the student's risk factors and protective factors;
>
> clearly identify any types of support that the student may need to continue his or her learning;
>
> establish the objectives of the SAP.

The Re-entry Meeting

The principal shall hold a meeting with school and board staff, the student, and, where possible, the student's parent(s) before the student returns to school. The purpose of this meeting is to facilitate the student's transition back to school by, for example, identifying and providing for any additional academic and non-academic support that the student may require upon returning to school. Where appropriate, community agency staff and any other significant persons or professionals may be involved in the re-entry planning.

Program Delivery

The delivery of the board program may take many forms, ranging from homework packages to attendance in a designated location at the discretion of the board.

Boards may enter into agreements with other boards for the provision of a program for students on long-term suspension. Coterminous boards should, wherever possible, collaborate on providing coordinated support to students on long-term suspension and their parents. Boards may also obtain or continue to obtain services from community agencies in the provision of the non-academic program component. These partnerships must respect collective agreements.

Accountability And Reporting Requirements

Boards must meet the following requirements:

> Boards must continue to collect data on suspensions and report on it to the ministry.
>
> Boards must establish performance indicators for monitoring, reviewing, and evaluating the effectiveness of the board program. These indicators should be developed in consultation with their school community, including principals, teachers, students, parents, school councils, their Special Education Advisory Committee, and their Parent Involvement Committee, as well as service providers in the community. Boards will also conduct a cyclical review of their programs in a timely manner.
>
> Boards must collect program data and share this data with the ministry, as required. Boards will also allow monitoring visits by the ministry, as required.
>
> Boards must enter into transfer payment agreements with the ministry. These agreements will outline requirements for board accountability and reporting.

Appendix: Excerpts From The Legislation

Education Act, as amended by the Education Amendment Act (Progressive Discipline and School Safety), 2007

Relevant excerpts from sections of the Education Act, as amended by the Education Amendment Act (Progressive Discipline and School Safety), 2007, are provided below for ease of reference.

SUSPENSION

Activities leading to possible suspension

306. (1) A principal shall consider whether to suspend a pupil if he or she believes that the pupil has engaged in any of the following activities while at school, at a school-related activity or in other circumstances where engaging in the activity will have an impact on the school climate:

1. Uttering a threat to inflict serious bodily harm on another person.
2. Possessing alcohol or illegal drugs.
3. Being under the influence of alcohol.
4. Swearing at a teacher or at another person in a position of authority.
5. Committing an act of vandalism that causes extensive damage to school property at the pupil's school or to property located on the premises of the pupil's school.
6. Bullying.
7. Any other activity that is an activity for which a principal may suspend a pupil under a policy of the board.

Factors principal must consider

(2) In considering whether to suspend a pupil for engaging in an activity described in subsection (1), a principal shall take into account any mitigating or other factors prescribed by the regulations.

Suspension

(3) If a principal decides to suspend a pupil for engaging in an activity described in subsection (1), the principal shall suspend the pupil from his or her school and from engaging in all school-related activities.

Duration of suspension

(4) A suspension under this section shall be for no less than one school day and no more than 20 school days and, in considering how long the suspension should be, a principal shall take into account any mitigating or other factors prescribed by the regulations.

Assignment to program, etc.

(5) When a principal suspends a pupil under this section, he or she shall assign the pupil to a program for suspended pupils in accordance with any policies or guidelines issued by the Minister.

Policies and guidelines

(6) The Minister may issue policies and guidelines to boards to assist principals in interpreting and administering this section.

School-related activities

(7) A pupil who is suspended is not considered to be engaged in school-related activities by virtue of participating in a program for suspended pupils.

Notice of suspension

308. (1) A principal who suspends a pupil under section 306 shall,

   a. inform the pupil's teacher of the suspension; and
   b. make all reasonable efforts to inform the pupil's parent or guardian of the suspension within 24 hours of the suspension being imposed, unless,
       i. the pupil is at least 18 years old, or
       ii. the pupil is 16 or 17 years old and has withdrawn from parental control.

Same

(2) A principal who suspends a pupil under section 306 shall ensure that written notice of the suspension is given promptly to the following persons:

   1. The pupil.
   2. The pupil's parent or guardian, unless,
       i. the pupil is at least 18 years old, or
       ii. the pupil is 16 or 17 years old and has withdrawn from parental control.

3. Such other persons as may be specified by board policy.

Contents of notice

(3) The notice under subsection (2) must include the following:

1. The reason for the suspension.
2. The duration of the suspension.
3. Information about any program for suspended pupils to which the pupil is assigned.

SUSPENSION, INVESTIGATION AND POSSIBLE EXPULSION

Activities leading to suspension

310. (1) A principal shall suspend a pupil if he or she believes that the pupil has engaged in any of the following activities while at school, at a school-related activity or in other circumstances where engaging in the activity will have an impact on the school climate:

1. Possessing a weapon, including possessing a firearm.
2, Using a weapon to cause or to threaten bodily harm to another person.
3. Committing physical assault on another person that causes bodily harm requiring treatment by a medical practitioner.
4. Committing sexual assault.
5. Trafficking in weapons or in illegal drugs.
6. Committing robbery.
7. Giving alcohol to a minor.
8. Any other activity that, under a policy of a board, is an activity for which a principal must suspend a pupil and, therefore in accordance with this Part, conduct an investigation to determine whether to recommend to the board that the pupil be expelled.

Same

(2) A pupil who is suspended under this section is suspended from his or her school and from engaging in all school-related activities.

Duration of suspension

(3) A principal may suspend a pupil under this section for up to 20 school days and, in considering how long the suspension should be, the principal shall take into account any mitigating or other factors prescribed by the regulations.

Assignment to program, etc.

(4) When a principal suspends a pupil under this section, he or she shall assign the pupil to a program for suspended pupils in accordance with any policies or guidelines issued by the Minister.

Notice of suspension

311. (1) A principal who suspends a pupil under section 310 shall,

    a. inform the pupil's teacher of the suspension; and

    b. make all reasonable efforts to inform the pupil's parent or guardian of the suspension within 24 hours of the suspension being imposed, unless,

        i. the pupil is at least 18 years old, or

        ii. the pupil is 16 or 17 years old and has withdrawn from parental control.

Same

(2) A principal who suspends a pupil under section 310 shall ensure that written notice of the suspension is given promptly to the following persons:

1. The pupil.
2. The pupil's parent or guardian, unless,
3. the pupil is at least 18 years old, or

    i. the pupil is 16 or 17 years old and has withdrawn from parental control.

    ii. Such other persons as may be specified by board policy.

Contents of notice

(3) The notice under subsection (2) must include the following:

1. The reason for the suspension.
2. The duration of the suspension.
3. Information about any program for suspended pupils to which the pupil is assigned.
4. Information about the investigation the principal will conduct under section 311.1 to determine whether to recommend that the pupil be expelled.
5. A statement indicating that,
    i. there is no immediate right to appeal the suspension,
    ii. if the principal does not recommend to the board that the pupil be expelled following the investigation under section 311.1, the suspension will become subject to appeal under section 311.2, and
    iii. if there is an expulsion hearing because the principal recommends to the board that the pupil be expelled, the suspension may be addressed by parties at the hearing.

Programs for suspended, expelled pupils

312. (1) Every board shall provide, in accordance with policies and guidelines issued by the Minister, if any,

a. at least one program for suspended pupils; and
b. at least one program for expelled pupils.

Policies and guidelines

(2) The Minister may establish policies and guidelines with respect to programs for suspended and expelled pupils and may,

a. impose different requirements on the provision of the programs for different circumstances, different locations or different classes of pupils;

b. set criteria respecting pupils' eligibility to participate in the programs and respecting the criteria to be met for successful completion of the programs;

c. require boards to offer plans to assist pupils who have successfully completed a program for expelled pupils with their transition back to school and to set criteria respecting those plans; and

d. authorize boards, subject to such conditions and restrictions as the Minister imposes, to enter into agreements with other boards for the provision of the programs.

Ontario Regulation 472/07, "Suspension and Expulsion of Pupils"

Relevant excerpts from Ontario Regulation 472/07, made under the Education Act, are provided below for ease of reference.

Mitigating factors

2. For the purposes of subsections 306 (2), 306 (4), 310 (3), 311.1 (4) and clauses 311.3 (7) (b) and 311.4 (2) (b) of the Act, the following mitigating factors shall be taken into account:

1. The pupil does not have the ability to control his or her behaviour.

2. The pupil does not have the ability to understand the foreseeable consequences of his or her behaviour.

3. The pupil's continuing presence in the school does not create an unacceptable risk to the safety of any person

Other factors

3. For the purposes of subsections 306 (2), 306 (4), 310 (3), 311.1 (4) and clauses 311.3 (7) (b) and 311.4 (2) (b) of the Act, the following other factors shall be taken into account if they would mitigate the seriousness of the activity for which the pupil may be or is being suspended or expelled:

1. The pupil's history.

2. Whether a progressive discipline approach has been used with the pupil.

3. Whether the activity for which the pupil may be or is being suspended or expelled was related to any harassment of the pupil

because of his or her race, ethnic origin, religion, disability, gender or sexual orientation or to any other harassment.

4. How the suspension or expulsion would affect the pupil's ongoing education.

5. The age of the pupil

6. In the case of a pupil for whom an individual education plan has been developed,

i. whether the behaviour was a manifestation of a disability identified in the pupil's individual education plan,

ii. whether appropriate individualized accommodation has been provided, and

iii. whether the suspension or expulsion is likely to result in an aggravation or worsening of the pupil's behaviour or conduct.

---

[1] In this memorandum, *student* refers to *pupil,* as used in the Education Act.

[2] In this memorandum, *school boards* and *boards* refer to district school boards and school authorities.

[3] This memorandum is informed by findings from programs currently available to students in Ontario; the Safe Schools Action Team's provincial consultations; a review of the Strict Discipline Programs; Model Projects to Promote Positive Student Behaviour initiative; and a review of the literature on practices in Ontario, other provinces, and a number of countries around the world.

[4] In this memorandum, *parent(s)* refers to parent(s) and guardian(s). Parental involvement applies, except in cases where the student is eighteen years of age or over or is sixteen or seventeen years of age and has "withdrawn from parental control".

[5] Community agencies include a range of community service agencies, local organizations, and programs.

[6] In this memorandum, principal refers to the principal or to a person designated by the principal or by the board.

APPENDIX C

Policy/Program Memorandum No. 142

Date of Issue:	August 23, 2007 **Effective:** Until revoked or modified
Subject:	SCHOOL BOARD PROGRAMS FOR EXPELLED STUDENTS
Application:	Directors of Education Superintendents of School Authorities Principals of Elementary Schools Principals of Secondary Schools Principals of Provincial Schools Special Education Advisory Committees
Reference:	The Education Act, as amended by the Education Amendment Act (Progressive Discipline and School Safety), 2007. Ontario Regulation 472/07, "Suspension and Expulsion of Pupils". Policy/Program Memorandum No. 141, "School Board Programs for Students on Long-Term Suspension", August 23, 2007.

Introduction

The Ministry of Education is committed to ensuring that all students[1] who are expelled have the opportunity to continue their education. The Education Act, as amended by the Education Amendment Act (Progressive Discipline and School Safety), 2007, requires school boards,[2] as of February 1, 2008, to:

> provide at least one program for students who have been expelled from all schools of the board;

> assign a student who has been expelled only from his or her school to another school of the board.

The purpose of this memorandum is to provide direction to school boards regarding the development of board programs for expelled students. For excerpts from the relevant sections of the Education Act and the regulation, see the Appendix to this memorandum.

With respect to programs for expelled students, research[3] has demonstrated that positive outcomes for students are related to specific program elements that are tailored to meet the needs of each student. In accordance with this memorandum, boards must establish programs that include the following elements:

> a planning meeting to determine the specific academic and non-academic program requirements

> a Student Action Plan (SAP) that outlines goals, objectives, and learning expectations, including provision for a review of the student's progress with regard to his or her SAP

> a re-entry plan to assist with the student's transition back to school and integration in the school

In the case of students with special education needs, boards are required to provide appropriate support consistent with the student's Individual Education Plan (IEP).

It is expected that boards will actively encourage expelled students to participate in the board program for expelled students. While boards cannot compel expelled students to participate in a board program for expelled students, students who wish to return to school must satisfy the objectives required for successful completion of a program for expelled students.

The active engagement of parents[4] and families and linkages to community agencies,[5] such as agencies that provide counselling support and addiction treatment, also contribute to positive overall outcomes for students.

Resources that are dedicated to programs for expelled students may also be used to benefit students who have not been expelled but who have shown behaviours that, if unchanged, could lead to an expulsion. However, the needs of expelled students remain the priority.

General Requirements

Suspension Pending Expulsion

A student who has been suspended pending an expulsion hearing shall be assigned to a board program for students on long-term suspension. See Policy/Program Memorandum No. 141, "School Board Programs for Students on Long-Term Suspension", August 23, 2007.

In accordance with Policy/Program Memorandum No. 141, an SAP will be developed for every student who makes a commitment to attend the board program for suspended students. The student and/or his or her parent(s) must notify the principal[6] verbally or in writing that the student wishes to attend the program. Once the principal has received this notification, development of the SAP must begin immediately. The SAP must be implemented as soon as possible. Every effort must be made to provide an opportunity for the student to maintain his or her regular academic course work throughout the suspension period.

Boards are also expected to provide a homework package for the student until the SAP is in place.

Expulsion

A student may be expelled either from his or her school only or from all schools of the board. If a student is expelled from his or her school only, he or she must be assigned to another school of the board.

If a student is expelled from all schools of the board, he or she must be assigned to a board program for expelled students. The student and/or his or her parent(s) must notify the principal verbally or in writing that the student is committed to attending the program. Once the principal has received this notification, development of the SAP must begin immediately.

In the notice of expulsion, parents must be provided with information on either the new school or the board program to which the expelled student has been assigned.

Where an expelled student who is transferred to another school requires additional support and resources, boards should make appropriate support available and/or facilitate the student's referral to community agencies.

Considerations for Program Development

In developing programs, boards have the flexibility to take into account local needs and circumstances, such as geographical considerations, demographics, cultural needs, and availability of board and community support and resources.

Boards should draw upon evidence-based practices that promote positive student behaviour. For example, the program should incorporate board-wide initiatives such as character development and bullying prevention.

In the development of board policies related to the creation of these programs, boards should consult with parents, principals, teachers, students, school councils, their Parent Involvement Committee, their Special Education Advisory Committee, community partners, social service agencies, members of Aboriginal communities (e.g., Elders), and those groups that are traditionally not consulted.

Boards must take into account the needs of individual students by showing sensitivity to diversity and to cultural needs in their programs for expelled students. Their programs should be in keeping with the relevant ministry policies on antiracism and ethnocultural equity and antidiscrimination education and with the principles in the ministry document *Ontario First Nation, Métis, and Inuit Education Policy Framework, 2007*.

Boards are required to adhere to the Municipal Freedom of Information and Protection of Privacy Act, the Ontario Human Rights Code, and the Education Act and regulations made under the Act in the development and implementation of programs. Boards should consult with their legal counsel and freedom of information coordinators to ensure that they are fulfilling their legal responsibilities.

School Board Policies on Program Operation

School boards are required to develop policies regarding the operation of their programs for students who are suspended or expelled. These policies must deal with, but are not limited to, the following issues:

> discipline (e.g., what constitutes unacceptable behaviour and the consequences of such behaviour)

> safety (e.g., what measures will be taken to ensure a safe learning and teaching environment)

Boards are expected to make their policies publicly available. Boards are also expected to provide their policies directly to students and their parents before and/or upon entry to a program for suspended or expelled students. In particular, students and their parents must be informed of the discipline and safety rules and the ways in which the rules will be implemented. Boards are advised to consult their legal counsel in the development of these policies, particularly on the aspects related to discipline and safety.

Program Requirements

Components of Programs for Expelled Students

Boards are responsible for determining the content and balance of the program for each student for both the academic and non-academic components of the program. The content and balance of the program for a student will depend on the needs of the student and the nature and severity of the behaviour that led to the expulsion.

Academic Component

The purpose of the academic component is to ensure that expelled students who are assigned to a board program have the opportunity to continue their education.

The academic component must follow the curriculum outlined in the Ontario curriculum policy documents, unless the student has an IEP that provides for modifications to the Ontario curriculum or an alternative program. The academic component may include, but is not limited to, the provision of distance learning, e-learning, remedial help in literacy and numeracy, individual instruction, and/or opportunities within the board.

Elementary school students must be supported in continuing to acquire the necessary knowledge and skills outlined in the Ontario curriculum policy documents for elementary schools.

Secondary school students must be supported in continuing to earn credits towards their Ontario Secondary School Diploma through such options as credit completion and credit recovery.

Non-academic Component

The purpose of the non-academic component is to assist expelled students in the development of long-term positive attitudes and behaviours by identifying and addressing the underlying causes of the behaviour that led to the expulsion.

Students may require a range of services and types of support that may include access to culturally appropriate support. The board should make appropriate support available and/or facilitate a student's referral to community agencies and/or provide support through other methods, such as remote access to resources (e.g., video conferencing, telepsychiatry). To meet the alternative programming requirements of a student with special education needs, the board should refer to the student's IEP.

Protocols between boards and community agencies should be in place to facilitate referral processes and the provision of services and support for students and their parents and families. Where such protocols already exist, they should be reviewed, and where they do not, new protocols should be developed to increase the board's capacity to respond to the needs of expelled students.

Developing and Implementing the Student Action Plan

An SAP must be developed for every expelled student who makes a commitment to attend the board program for expelled students (see page 3 under "Expulsion"). The SAP will be developed on the basis of the information gathered at a planning meeting (see below). The SAP should build on the SAP that was developed for the student while he or she was on a long-term suspension pending expulsion, if the student attended the board program for suspended students.

The SAP will be developed by the principal in cooperation with appropriate staff, the student, and his or her parent(s). It is important that parents participate in the development and implementation of the SAP on an ongoing basis. Boards should make reasonable efforts to enable parents to participate by, for example, reaching out to community members who can provide translation services for those whose first language is not English or French.

It is the responsibility of the board to coordinate the types of support required to assist the student in continuing his or her learning. For students with special education needs, boards are required to provide appropriate support consistent with the student's IEP.

The Planning Meeting

Once the student and/or his or her parent(s) have indicated that the student is committed to attending the program, the principal shall hold a planning meeting. The planning meeting should be a collaborative process and must include school and board staff and the student. Where possible, the student's parent(s) or other significant family member(s), as well as the student's teacher(s), should also be present at the meeting. Principals should make reasonable efforts to include parents in this meeting. If the parents cannot be present, the planning meeting should proceed nevertheless, and the principal must attempt to follow up with the parent(s) of the student as soon after the meeting as possible. In addition, where appropriate, community agency staff and any other relevant persons or professionals should also be included in the planning meeting.

The purpose of the planning meeting is to:

>identify the needs of the student and determine whether any assessment is required;
>
>identify the student's risk factors and protective factors;
>
>describe the types of support and services required to assist the student in achieving the goals of the academic and non-academic components (e.g., career development counselling, use of mentors from appropriate communities).

The following information should be considered during the planning meeting and should be used to develop the SAP:

>the student's history
>
>the student's learning experiences from any long-term suspension program that he or she may have attended
>
>the student's strengths
>
>the nature and severity of the behaviour that led to the expulsion, including any mitigating or other factors
>
>information from anyone who has provided a specialized service (e.g., a speech therapist)
>
>information from other sources who have helped or are expected to help the student, including culturally appropriate support persons

All relevant information on the student, including existing documentation (e.g., current assessments, the IEP), should be considered while complying with all legal and statutory requirements and privacy laws.

Development and Review of the Student Action Plan

The SAP must contain both an academic and non-academic component. For both the academic and non-academic components, the SAP must outline:

>   goals, objectives, and learning expectations;

>   measures of success;

>   strategies and types of support.

The SAP should be reviewed on a regular basis to determine the student's progress in meeting the stated objectives in both the academic and the non-academic components of the plan. When a student enters a program for expelled students, all parties, including the student, must be made aware of the process for determining when the student has satisfied the objectives required for successful completion of the program and is therefore eligible to be readmitted to a school of the board. The student and/or his or her parent(s) should be involved in the review of the SAP.

Information on the person who is designated by the board to be responsible for overseeing the student's readmission should also be included in the SAP.

Development of a Plan for Re-entry to School

A student who has been expelled from all schools of a board and/or his or her parent(s) may apply in writing to a person designated by the board requesting that the student be readmitted to a school of that board. For a student who has been expelled from only one school of a board, and where the student and/or his or her parent(s) wish that the student return to his or her original school, the student and/or his or her parent(s) may apply in writing to a person designated by the board requesting that the student be reassigned to the school.

When the student has successfully met the objectives of the program for expelled students, as outlined in the SAP, the student must be readmitted to school. The person who has provided the program must determine whether an expelled student has successfully completed a program for expelled students, or has satisfied the objectives required for successful completion of a program for expelled students.

When a student is considered ready to be readmitted to school, a re-entry plan must be developed as part of the SAP to assist with the student's transition and integration back into the school.

As part of the development of the re-entry plan, the board must hold a meeting that includes board staff, staff of the school to which the student is seeking readmission, and the student. Where possible, the student's parent(s) or other significant family member(s), as well as the student's teacher(s), should also be present. Principals should make reasonable efforts to include parents in this meeting. If the parents cannot be present, the planning meeting should proceed nevertheless, and the principal must attempt to follow up with the parent(s) of the student as soon after the meeting as possible. In addition, where appropriate, community agency staff and any other relevant persons or professionals should also be included in the meeting.

The re-entry plan should contain the following elements:

> description of the re-entry process for successful transition back to school
>
> identification of the types of support in both the academic and non-academic components that are needed to sustain student learning

Program Delivery

Boards may enter into agreements with other boards for the provision of a program for students who are expelled from all schools of a board. Coterminous boards should, wherever possible, collaborate on providing coordinated support to expelled students and their parents. Boards may also obtain or continue to obtain services from community agencies in the provision of the non-academic program component. These partnerships must respect collective agreements.

Accountability And Reporting Requirements

Boards must meet the following requirements:

> Boards must continue to collect data on expulsions and report on it to the ministry.

Boards must establish performance indicators for monitoring, reviewing, and evaluating the effectiveness of the board program. These indicators should be developed in consultation with their school community, including principals, teachers, students, parents, school councils, their Special Education Advisory Committee, and their Parent Involvement Committee, as well as service providers in the community. Boards will also conduct a cyclical review of their programs in a timely manner.

Boards must collect program data and share this data with the ministry, as required. Boards will also allow monitoring visits by the ministry, as required.

Boards must enter into transfer payment agreements with the ministry. These agreements will outline requirements for board accountability and reporting.

Appendix: Excerpts From The Legislation

Education Act, as amended by the Education Amendment Act (Progressive Discipline and School Safety), 2007

Relevant excerpts from sections of the Education Act, as amended by the Education Amendment Act (Progressive Discipline and School Safety), 2007, are provided below for ease of reference.

SUSPENSION, INVESTIGATION AND POSSIBLE EXPULSION

Activities leading to suspension

310. (1) A principal shall suspend a pupil if he or she believes that the pupil has engaged in any of the following activities while at school, at a school-related activity or in other circumstances where engaging in the activity will have an impact on the school climate:

1. Possessing a weapon, including possessing a firearm.

2. Using a weapon to cause or to threaten bodily harm to another person.

3. Committing physical assault on another person that causes bodily harm requiring treatment by a medical practitioner.

4. Committing sexual assault.
5. Trafficking in weapons or in illegal drugs.
6. Committing robbery.
7. Giving alcohol to a minor.
8. Any other activity that, under a policy of a board, is an activity for which a principal must suspend a pupil and, therefore in accordance with this Part, conduct an investigation to determine whether to recommend to the board that the pupil be expelled.

Same

(2) A pupil who is suspended under this section is suspended from his or her school and from engaging in all school-related activities.

Duration of suspension

(3) A principal may suspend a pupil under this section for up to 20 school days and, in considering how long the suspension should be, the principal shall take into account any mitigating or other factors prescribed by the regulations.

Assignment to program, etc.

(4) When a principal suspends a pupil under this section, he or she shall assign the pupil to a program for suspended pupils in accordance with any policies or guidelines issued by the Minister.

Notice of suspension

311. (1) A principal who suspends a pupil under section 310 shall,
 a. inform the pupil's teacher of the suspension; and
 b. make all reasonable efforts to inform the pupil's parent or guardian of the suspension within 24 hours of the suspension being imposed, unless,
  i. the pupil is at least 18 years old, or
  ii. the pupil is 16 or 17 years old and has withdrawn from parental control.

Same

(2) A principal who suspends a pupil under section 310 shall ensure that written notice of the suspension is given promptly to the following persons:

1. The pupil.
2. The pupil's parent or guardian, unless,
    i. the pupil is at least 18 years old, or
    ii. the pupil is 16 or 17 years old and has withdrawn from parental control.
3. Such other persons as may be specified by board policy.

Contents of notice

(3) The notice under subsection (2) must include the following:

1. The reason for the suspension.
2. The duration of the suspension.
3. Information about any program for suspended pupils to which the pupil is assigned.
4. Information about the investigation the principal will conduct under section 311.1 to determine whether to recommend that the pupil be expelled.
5. A statement indicating that,
    i. there is no immediate right to appeal the suspension,
    ii. if the principal does not recommend to the board that the pupil be expelled following the investigation under section 311.1, the suspension will become subject to appeal under section 311.2, and
    iii. if there is an expulsion hearing because the principal recommends to the board that the pupil be expelled, the suspension may be addressed by parties at the hearing.

Investigation following suspension

311.1 (1) When a pupil is suspended under section 310, the principal shall conduct an investigation to determine whether to recommend to the board that the pupil be expelled.

If expulsion recommended: report

(7) If, on concluding the investigation, the principal decides to recommend to the board that the pupil be expelled, he or she shall prepare a report that contains the following:

1. A summary of the principal's findings.
2. The principal's recommendation as to whether the pupil should be expelled from his or her school only or from all schools of the board.
3. The principal's recommendation as to,
   i. the type of school that might benefit the pupil, if the pupil is expelled from his or her school only, or
   ii. the type of program for expelled pupils that might benefit the pupil, if the pupil is expelled from all schools of the board.

Written notice

(9) The principal shall ensure that written notice containing the following is given to every person to whom the principal was required to give notice of the suspension under section 311 at the same time as the principal's report is provided to that person:

4. Detailed information about the procedures and possible outcomes of the expulsion hearing, including, but not limited to, information explaining that,
   i. if the board expels the pupil from his or her school only, the board will assign the pupil to another school, and
   ii. if the board expels the pupil from all schools of the board, the board will assign the pupil to a program for expelled pupils.

Decision

311.3 (6) After completing the hearing, the board shall decide,

    a. whether to expel the pupil; and

    b. if the pupil is to be expelled, whether the pupil is expelled from his or her school only or from all schools of the board.

If pupil expelled

311.5 If a board expels a pupil, the board shall assign the pupil to,

    a. in the case of a pupil expelled from his or her school only, another school of the board; and

    b. in the case of a pupil expelled from all schools of the board, a program for expelled pupils.

Notice of expulsion

311.6 (1) A board that expels a pupil shall ensure that written notice of the expulsion is given promptly to,

    a. all the parties to the expulsion hearing; and

    b. the pupil, if the pupil was not a party to the expulsion hearing.

Contents of notice

(2) The notice under subsection (1) must include the following:

1. The reason for the expulsion.
2. A statement indicating whether the pupil is expelled from his or her school only or from all schools of the board.
3. Information about the school or program for expelled pupils to which the pupil is assigned.
4. Information about the right to appeal under section 311.7, including the steps that must be taken to appeal.

Programs for suspended, expelled pupils

312. (1) Every board shall provide, in accordance with policies and guidelines issued by the Minister, if any,

1. at least one program for suspended pupils; and
2. at least one program for expelled pupils.

Policies and guidelines

(2) The Minister may establish policies and guidelines with respect to programs for suspended and expelled pupils and may,

- a. impose different requirements on the provision of the programs for different circumstances, different locations or different classes of pupils;
- b. set criteria respecting pupils' eligibility to participate in the programs and respecting the criteria to be met for successful completion of the programs;
- c. require boards to offer plans to assist pupils who have successfully completed a program for expelled pupils with their transition back to school and to set criteria respecting those plans; and
- d. authorize boards, subject to such conditions and restrictions as the Minister imposes, to enter into agreements with other boards for the provision of the programs.

Status of expelled pupil

313. (1) An expelled pupil continues to be a pupil of the board that expelled him or her if the pupil attends a program for expelled pupils,

- a. offered by that board; or
- b. offered by another board under an agreement between that board and the board that expelled the pupil.

Same

(2) An expelled pupil ceases to be a pupil of the board that expelled him or her if,

- a. the pupil is assigned by that board to a program for expelled pupils and does not attend the program; or
- b. the pupil registers as a pupil of another board.

Powers of other board

314. (1) If a pupil who has been expelled from one board registers as a pupil of another board, the other board may,

   a. assign the pupil to a school of that board; or

   b. assign the pupil to a program for expelled pupils, unless the pupil satisfies the requirements of clause 314.1 (1) (a) or (b) as determined by a person who provides a program for expelled pupils.

Clarification

(2) If the other board assigns the expelled pupil to a school without knowing that he or she has been expelled by another board, the board may subsequently remove the pupil from the school and assign him or her to a program for expelled pupils, subject to the following conditions:

1. The board must assign the pupil to a program for expelled pupils promptly on learning that he or she has been expelled from another board.

2. The board shall not assign the pupil to a program for expelled pupils if the pupil satisfies the requirements of clause 314.1 (1) (a) or (b) as determined by a person who provides a program for expelled pupils.

Return to school after expulsion

314.1 (1) A pupil who has been expelled from all schools of a board is entitled to be readmitted to a school of the board if the pupil has, since being expelled,

   a. successfully completed a program for expelled pupils; or

   b. satisfied the objectives required for the successful completion of a program for expelled pupils.

Determination

(2) The determination of whether an expelled pupil satisfies the requirements of clause (1) (a) or (b) is to be made by a person who provides a program for expelled pupils.

Board must readmit pupil

(3) An expelled pupil may apply in writing to a person designated by the board that expelled him or her to be readmitted to a school of that board and, if the pupil satisfies the requirements of clause (1) (a) or (b) as determined by a person who provides a program for expelled pupils, the board shall,

   a. readmit the expelled pupil to a school of the board; and

   b. promptly inform the pupil in writing of his or her readmittance.

Clarification: successful completion of program

314.2 A pupil who has successfully completed a program for expelled pupils provided by any board or person under this Part has satisfied the requirements of clause 314.1 (1) (a), and no board shall,

   a. require the pupil to attend a program for expelled pupils provided by that board before being admitted to a school of the board; or

   b. refuse to admit the pupil on the basis that the pupil completed a program for expelled pupils provided by another board or person.

Return to original school after expulsion

314.3 A pupil who has been expelled from one school of a board but not from all schools of the board may apply in writing to a person designated by the board to be re-assigned to the school from which he or she was expelled.

Clarification: resident pupils

314.4 For greater certainty, nothing in this Part requires a board to admit or readmit a pupil who is not otherwise qualified to be a resident pupil of the board.

Ontario Regulation 472/07, "Suspension and Expulsion of Pupils"

Relevant excerpts from Ontario Regulation 472/07, made under the Education Act, are provided below for ease of reference.

Mitigating factors

2. For the purposes of subsections 306 (2), 306 (4), 310 (3), 311.1 (4) and clauses 311.3 (7) (b) and 311.4 (2) (b) of the Act, the following mitigating factors shall be taken into account:

1. The pupil does not have the ability to control his or her behaviour.
2. The pupil does not have the ability to understand the foreseeable consequences of his or her behaviour.
3. The pupil's continuing presence in the school does not create an unacceptable risk to the safety of any person.

Other factors

3. For the purposes of subsections 306 (2), 306 (4), 310 (3), 311.1 (4) and clauses 311.3 (7) (b) and 311.4 (2) (b) of the Act, the following other factors shall be taken into account if they would mitigate the seriousness of the activity for which the pupil may be or is being suspended or expelled:

1. The pupil's history.
2. Whether a progressive discipline approach has been used with the pupil.
3. Whether the activity for which the pupil may be or is being suspended or expelled was related to any harassment of the pupil because of his or her race, ethnic origin, religion, disability, gender or sexual orientation or to any other harassment.
4. How the suspension or expulsion would affect the pupil's ongoing education.
5. The age of the pupil.
6. In the case of a pupil for whom an individual education plan has been developed,
    i. whether the behaviour was a manifestation of a disability identified in the pupil's individual education plan,
    ii. whether appropriate individualized accommodation has been provided, and
    iii. whether the suspension or expulsion is likely to result in an aggravation or worsening of the pupil's behaviour or conduct.

[1] In this memorandum, *student* refers to *pupil*, as used in the Education Act. *Expelled student* refers to a student who has been expelled from his or her school only or from all schools of a board.

[2] In this memorandum, *school boards* and *boards* refer to district school boards and school authorities.

[3] This memorandum is informed by findings from programs currently available to students in Ontario; the Safe Schools Action Team's provincial consultations; a review of the Strict Discipline Programs; Model Projects to Promote Positive Student Behaviour initiative; and a review of the literature on practices in Ontario, other provinces, and a number of countries around the world.

[4] In this memorandum, *parent(s)* refers to parent(s) and guardian(s). Parental involvement applies, except in cases where the student is eighteen years of age or over or is sixteen or seventeen years of age and has "withdrawn from parental control".

[5] Community agencies include a range of community service agencies, local organizations, and programs.

[6] In this memorandum, *principal* refers to the principal or to a person designated by the principal or by the board.

Appendix D

Policy/Program Memorandum No. 144

Date of Issue: October 4, 2007	**Effective:** Until revoked or modified
Subject:	**BULLYING PREVENTION AND INTERVENTION**
Application:	Directors of Education Superintendents of School Authorities Principals of Elementary Schools Principals of Secondary Schools Principals of Provincial Schools Special Education Advisory Committees
Reference:	The Education Act, as amended by the Education Amendment Act (Progressive Discipline and School Safety), 2007. Ontario Regulation 472/07, "Suspension and Expulsion of Pupils".

Introduction

School boards[1] in Ontario are required to develop and implement policies on bullying prevention and intervention, and are required to have their policies in place by February 1, 2008. Boards that already have bullying prevention and intervention policies in place must review their existing policies and any other relevant board policies to ensure that they are consistent with the policies in this memorandum.

The purpose of this memorandum is to provide direction to boards on the development and implementation of their policies on bullying prevention and intervention.

Providing students[2] with an opportunity to learn and develop in a safe and respectful society is a shared responsibility in which school boards and schools play an important role. Schools that have bullying prevention and intervention strategies foster a positive learning and teaching environment that supports academic achievement for all students and that helps students reach their full potential.

A positive "school climate is a crucial component of prevention; it may be defined as the sum total of all of the personal relationships within a school. When these relationships are founded in mutual acceptance and inclusion, and modelled by all, a culture of respect becomes the norm."[3] A positive school climate exists when all members of the school community feel safe, comfortable, and accepted. To help achieve a positive environment in their schools, boards and schools should actively promote and support positive behaviours that reflect their character development initiatives. They should also endeavour to ensure that parents[4] and members of the broader community are involved in the school community.

Boards should support and maintain a positive school climate in their schools. The following are some characteristics of a positive school climate:[5]

>Students and staff feel safe and are safe.

>Healthy and inclusive relationships are promoted.

>Students are encouraged to be positive leaders in their school community.

>All partners are actively engaged.

>Bullying prevention messages are reinforced through programs addressing discrimination based on such factors as age, race, sexual orientation, gender, faith, disability, ethnicity, and socio-economic disadvantage.

>Improvement of learning outcomes for all students is emphasized.

In recognition of the importance of addressing bullying, which can have a significant impact on student safety, learning, and the school climate, bullying has been added to the list of infractions for which suspension must be considered. With the passage of the Education Amendment Act (Progressive Discipline and School Safety), 2007, this change comes into effect February 1, 2008. For the relevant sections of the Education Act and Ontario Regulation 472/07, see the excerpts provided in the Appendix to this memorandum.

Research

Research and experience show that bullying is a serious issue that has far-reaching consequences for individuals, their families and peers, and the community at large. According to the Centre for Addiction and Mental Health, one-third of students are being bullied at school and almost a third of students report having bullied someone else.[6] Research indicates that a clearly articulated school-wide bullying prevention policy is the foundation of effective bullying prevention programming.

If students who are bullied, who bully others, or who witness bullying receive the necessary support, they can learn effective strategies for interacting positively with others and for promoting positive peer dynamics. Research also shows that administrators and teachers need to be provided with opportunities to acquire the knowledge and skills necessary to address bullying through school-level bullying prevention and intervention strategies.

Definition of *Bullying*

For the purposes of developing and implementing policies on bullying prevention and intervention, boards will use the following definition of *bullying*:

Bullying is typically a form of repeated, persistent, and aggressive behaviour directed at an individual or individuals that is intended to cause (or should be known to cause) fear and distress and/or harm to another person's body, feelings, self-esteem, or reputation. Bullying occurs in a context where there is a real or perceived power imbalance.

Students may attain or maintain power over others in the school through real or perceived differences. Some areas of difference may be size, strength, age, intelligence, economic status, social status, solidarity of peer group, religion, ethnicity, disability, need for special education, sexual orientation, family circumstances, gender, and race.

Bullying is a dynamic of unhealthy interaction that can take many forms. It can be physical (e.g., hitting, pushing, tripping), verbal (e.g., name calling, mocking, or making sexist, racist, or homophobic comments), or social (e.g., excluding others from a group, spreading gossip or rumours). It may also occur through the use of technology (e.g., spreading rumours, images, or hurtful comments through the use of e-mail, cellphones, text messaging, Internet websites, or other technology).

Children who suffer prolonged victimization through bullying, as well as children who use power and aggression as bullies, may experience a range of psycho-social problems that may extend into adolescence and adulthood.

School Board Policies on Bullying Prevention and Intervention

Policy Development

In developing their policies, boards have the flexibility to take into account local needs and circumstances, such as geographical considerations, demographics, cultural needs, and availability of board and community support and resources.

Boards should draw upon evidence-based practices that promote positive student behaviour. In the development of their policies, boards must consult with school councils. They should also consult with parents, principals,[7] teachers, students, their Parent Involvement Committee, their Special Education Advisory Committee, community partners, social service agencies, members of Aboriginal communities (e.g., Elders), and those groups that are traditionally not consulted.

Boards must take into account the needs of individual students by showing sensitivity to diversity, to cultural needs, and to special education needs in their policies, in keeping with the relevant ministry policies on antiracism and ethnocultural equity and antidiscrimination education and with the principles in the ministry document *Ontario First Nation, Métis, and Inuit Education Policy Framework, 2007*. Where possible, the policies should incorporate other relevant board-wide policies, strategies, and initiatives, such as Student Success and character development.

Boards are required to adhere to the Municipal Freedom of Information and Protection of Privacy Act, the Ontario Human Rights Code, and the Education Act and regulations made under the Act in the development and implementation of their policies. Board policies must respect all applicable collective agreements. Boards should consult with their legal counsel and freedom of information coordinators to ensure that they are fulfilling their legal responsibilities.

Policy Components and Implementation Strategies

1. Policy Statement

Board policies must include the following statements:

> Bullying adversely affects students' ability to learn.
>
> Bullying adversely affects healthy relationships and the school climate.
>
> Bullying adversely affects a school's ability to educate its students.
>
> Bullying will not be accepted on school property, at school-related activities, on school buses, or in any other circumstances (e.g., online) where engaging in bullying will have a negative impact on the school climate.

2. The Definition of Bullying

Board policies must include the definition of bullying that is contained in this memorandum.

3. Prevention Strategies

Board policies must include a comprehensive prevention strategy that includes expectations for appropriate student behaviour.

Board policies should include teaching strategies that support the school-wide bullying prevention policies. These strategies should focus on developing healthy relationships by including bullying prevention in daily classroom teaching (e.g., by including books that deal with bullying on reading lists).

School boards should provide opportunities for all students to participate in bullying prevention training and leadership initiatives within their own school.

4. Intervention Strategies

Board policies must include a comprehensive intervention strategy to address incidents of bullying, including appropriate and timely responses. Intervention should be done in ways that are consistent with a progressive discipline approach. The strategies could range from early interventions to more intensive interventions in cases of persistent bullying, with possible referral to community or social service agencies. Ongoing interventions may be necessary to sustain and promote positive student behaviour.

Boards must also put in place procedures to allow students to report bullying incidents safely and in a way that will minimize the possibility of reprisal. These procedures should also define the responsibilities and roles of the principal, teachers, parents, and students.

Boards must provide support for students who have been bullied, students who have bullied others, and students who have been affected by observing bullying.

Board policies should include teaching strategies that support a comprehensive intervention strategy. These strategies should focus on developing healthy relationships by including bullying prevention throughout the curriculum in daily classroom teaching.

5. Training Strategies for Members of the School Community

Boards must put in place training strategies for all administrators, teachers, and educational assistants on bullying prevention and intervention, including training on cultural sensitivity and on respect for diversity and special education needs. Boards may also make training available to other adults who have significant contact with students (e.g., other school staff, school bus operators/drivers, volunteers). Boards should also recognize the ongoing need to support training for new teachers and support staff.

6. Communication and Outreach Strategies

Boards must actively communicate their policies and procedures on bullying prevention and intervention, as well as the definition of *bullying*, to students, parents, teachers and other school staff, school councils, volunteers, and school bus operators/drivers.

It is important that the roles and responsibilities of all members of the school community (e.g., principals, teachers, students, parents) be clearly articulated and understood.

Boards should make every effort to share this information with parents whose first language is a language other than English or French.

7. Monitoring and Review

Boards must establish a monitoring and review process to determine the effectiveness of their bullying prevention and intervention policies and procedures. This process should include the following:

> an analysis of the school climate through anonymous surveys of students, staff members, and parents provided by their schools (these surveys should be done on a regular cycle, as determined by the board)
>
> performance indicators for monitoring, reviewing, and evaluating the effectiveness of the board's bullying prevention and intervention policies

School-Level Plans

School boards must require that all their schools develop and implement school-wide bullying prevention and intervention plans as part of their School Improvement Plan. Components of these plans must include the following:[8]

> the definition of *bullying*
>
> prevention strategies
>
> intervention strategies
>
> training strategies for members of the school community
>
> communication and outreach strategies
>
> monitoring and review processes

The school plans must be consistent with the policies in this memorandum and with the policies and procedures of the board.

Safe Schools Teams

Each school must have in place a safe schools team responsible for school safety that is composed of at least one student (where appropriate), one parent, one teacher, one support staff member, one community partner, and the principal. The team must have a staff chair. An existing school committee (e.g., healthy schools committee) can assume this role.

Appendix: Excerpts From the Legislation

Education Act, as amended by the Education Amendment Act (Progressive Discipline and School Safety), 2007

Relevant excerpts from sections 301, 302, and 306 of the Education Act, as amended by the Education Amendment Act (Progressive Discipline and School Safety), 2007, are provided below for ease of reference. Note that the Act now adds bullying to the list of infractions for which suspension must be considered.

Policies and guidelines promoting safety

301. (7) The Minister may establish policies and guidelines to promote the safety of pupils.

Duty of boards

(9) The Minister may require boards to comply with policies and guidelines established under this section.

Board's policies and guidelines promoting safety

302. (3) If required to do so by the Minister, a board shall establish policies and guidelines to promote the safety of pupils, and the policies and guidelines must be consistent with those established by the Minister under section 301 and must address such matters and include such requirements as the Minister may specify.

Suspension

Activities leading to possible suspension

306. (1) A principal shall consider whether to suspend a pupil if he or she believes that the pupil has engaged in any of the following activities while at school, at a school-related activity or in other circumstances where engaging in the activity will have an impact on the school climate:

1. Uttering a threat to inflict serious bodily harm on another person.
2. Possessing alcohol or illegal drugs.

3. Being under the influence of alcohol.
4. Swearing at a teacher or at another person in a position of authority.
5. Committing an act of vandalism that causes extensive damage to school property at the pupil's school or to property located on the premises of the pupil's school.
6. **Bullying**.
7. Any other activity that is an activity for which a principal may suspend a pupil under a policy of the board.

Factors principal must consider

(2) In considering whether to suspend a pupil for engaging in an activity described in subsection (1), a principal shall take into account any mitigating or other factors prescribed by the regulations.

Ontario Regulation 472/07, "Suspension and Expulsion of Pupils"

Relevant excerpts from Ontario Regulation 472/07, made under the Education Act, are provided below for ease of reference.

Mitigating factors

2. For the purposes of subsections 306 (2), 306 (4), 310 (3), 311.1 (4) and clauses 311.3 (7) (b) and 311.4 (2) (b) of the Act, the following mitigating factors shall be taken into account:

1. The pupil does not have the ability to control his or her behaviour.
2. The pupil does not have the ability to understand the foreseeable consequences of his or her behaviour.
3. The pupil's continuing presence in the school does not create an unacceptable risk to the safety of any person.

Other factors

3. For the purposes of subsections 306 (2), 306 (4), 310 (3), 311.1 (4) and clauses 311.3 (7) (b) and 311.4 (2) (b) of the Act, the following other factors shall be taken into account if they would mitigate the seriousness of the activity for which the pupil may be or is being suspended or expelled:

1. The pupil's history.
2. Whether a progressive discipline approach has been used with the pupil.
3. Whether the activity for which the pupil may be or is being suspended or expelled was related to any harassment of the pupil because of his or her race, ethnic origin, religion, disability, gender or sexual orientation or to any other harassment.
4. How the suspension or expulsion would affect the pupil's ongoing education.
5. The age of the pupil.
6. In the case of a pupil for whom an individual education plan has been developed,
    i. whether the behaviour was a manifestation of a disability identified in the pupil's individual education plan,
    ii. whether appropriate individualized accommodation has been provided, and
    iii. whether the suspension or expulsion is likely to result in an aggravation or worsening of the pupil's behaviour or conduct.

---

[1] In this memorandum, *school board(s)* and *board(s)* refer to district school boards and school authorities.

[2] The term *student*, as used in this memorandum, refers to *pupil*, as used in the Education Act.

[3] *Safe Schools Policy and Practice: An Agenda for Action*, Report of the Safe Schools Action Team (Toronto: June 2006), p. 8.

[4] In this memorandum, *parent(s)* refers to parent(s) and guardian(s). Parental involvement applies, except in cases where the student is eighteen years of age or over or is sixteen or seventeen years of age and has "withdrawn from parental control".

[5] Based on *Safe Schools Policy and Practice: An Agenda for Action*, Report of the Safe Schools Action Team (Toronto: June 2006), p. 7.

[6] Edward M. Adlaf, Angela Paglia-Boak, Joseph H. Beitchman, and David Wolfe, *The Mental Health and Well-Being of Ontario Students, 1991-2005*. Ontario Student Drug Use Survey, CAMH Research Document Series, No. 18 (Toronto: Centre for Addiction and Mental Health, 2005), p. 89.

[7] In this memorandum, *principal* refers to the principal or to a person designated by the principal or by the board.

[8] *Shaping Safer Schools: A Bullying Prevention Action Plan*, Report of the Safe Schools Action Team (November 2005), pp. 24–27.

APPENDIX E

Policy/Program Memorandum No. 145

Date of Issue:	October 4, 2007 **Effective:** Until revoked or modified
Subject:	**PROGRESSIVE DISCIPLINE AND PROMOTING POSITIVE STUDENT BEHAVIOUR**
Application:	Directors of Education Superintendents of School Authorities Principals of Elementary Schools Principals of Secondary Schools Principals of Provincial Schools Special Education Advisory Committees
Reference:	The Education Act, as amended by the Education Amendment Act (Progressive Discipline and School Safety), 2007. Ontario Regulation 472/07, "Suspension and Expulsion of Pupils".

Introduction

The Ministry of Education is committed to building and sustaining a positive school climate for all students[1] in order to support their education so that all students reach their full potential. School boards[2] are required to develop and implement policies on progressive discipline and are required to have their policies in place by February 1, 2008. Boards that already have a progressive discipline policy in place must review their existing policy to ensure that it meets all of the requirements set out in this memorandum.

The purpose of this memorandum is to provide direction to boards on the development and implementation of their policies on progressive discipline.

Background

On June 4, 2007, the Education Amendment Act (Progressive Discipline and School Safety), 2007, was passed, amending Part XIII of the Education Act dealing with behaviour, discipline, and safety. Changes to the safe schools provisions of the Act more effectively combine discipline with opportunities for students to continue their education. These amendments come into force on February 1, 2008. For excerpts from the relevant sections of the Education Act and Ontario Regulation 472/07, see the Appendix to this memorandum.

The changes to the safe schools provisions of the Act provide the opportunity for students who have been expelled or those on a long-term suspension to continue their education by requiring school boards to provide programs for these students. The ministry provides direction to boards to support this legislative requirement in Policy/Program Memoranda Nos. 141 and 142.[3]

The Act requires that mitigating and other factors be taken into account when considering whether to suspend or expel a student. These factors are described in Ontario Regulation 472/07, "Suspension and Expulsion of Pupils" (for relevant excerpts, see the Appendix to this memorandum). In the case of suspension pending expulsion, mitigating and other factors are only to be taken into account in determining the duration of the suspension.

As part of the legislative changes, bullying has been added to the list of infractions for which suspension must be considered. The policy memorandum on bullying prevention and intervention[4] requires every school board and school in Ontario to develop and implement a policy on bullying prevention and intervention. The memorandum provides direction to boards on the development and implementation of board policies on bullying prevention and intervention. It emphasizes the importance of addressing bullying, which can have a significant impact on student safety, learning, and school climate.

Amendments to the safe schools provisions of the Act support the ministry's Safe Schools Strategy, which places an emphasis on prevention strategies that promote and support positive student behaviour and early and ongoing intervention.

Promoting and Supporting Positive Student Behaviour

The ministry acknowledges the importance of actively promoting and supporting appropriate and positive student behaviours that contribute to and sustain a safe learning and teaching environment in which every student can reach his or her full potential. Linkages to ministry initiatives such as character development and the Student Success Strategy are key in promoting and supporting appropriate and positive student behaviours.

Prevention

Prevention is the establishment and use of programs such as bullying prevention and citizenship development, as well as other positive activities designed to promote the building of healthy relationships and appropriate behaviours.[5]

Generally, prevention measures and initiatives include the whole school and all aspects of school life. Schools that have prevention and intervention strategies foster a positive school climate that supports academic achievement for all students. Boards and schools should focus on prevention and early intervention as the key to maintaining a positive school environment in which students can learn.

A positive "school climate is a crucial component of prevention; it may be defined as the sum total of all of the personal relationships within a school. When these relationships are founded in mutual acceptance and inclusion, and modelled by all, a culture of respect becomes the norm."[6] A positive climate exists when all members of the school community feel safe, comfortable, and accepted.

Programs and activities that focus on the building of healthy relationships, character development, and peer relations provide the foundation for an effective continuum of strategies within a school and school-related activities. These supportive strategies and empowerment programs are the basis for creating a positive school climate.

In addition to teachers and administrators, other staff such as educational assistants, Native education counsellors, social workers, child and youth workers, psychologists, and attendance counsellors all play an important role in supporting students and contributing to a positive learning and teaching environment. A positive school climate also includes the participation of the school community, including parents,[7] as well as the broader community, which can have a major impact on the success of all students in the school.

Progressive Discipline

Progressive discipline is a whole-school approach that utilizes a continuum of interventions, supports, and consequences to address inappropriate student behaviour and to build upon strategies that promote positive behaviours described above. When inappropriate behaviour occurs, disciplinary measures should be applied within a framework that shifts the focus from one that is solely punitive to one that is both corrective and supportive. Schools should utilize a range of interventions, supports, and consequences that include learning opportunities for reinforcing positive behaviour while helping students to make good choices.

In some circumstances, short-term suspension may be a useful tool. In the case of a serious incident, long-term suspension or expulsion, which is further along the continuum of progressive discipline, may be the response that is required.

For students with special education needs, interventions, supports, and consequences must be consistent with the student's strengths, needs, goals, and expectations contained in his or her Individual Education Plan (IEP).

Schools are expected to actively engage parents in the progressive discipline approach.

A progressive discipline approach includes the use of early and ongoing intervention strategies and strategies to address inappropriate behaviour, which are described below.

Early and Ongoing Intervention Strategies

Early and ongoing intervention strategies will help prevent unsafe or inappropriate behaviours in a school and in school-related activities. Intervention strategies should provide students with appropriate supports that address inappropriate behaviour and that would result in an improved school climate. For example, early interventions may include, but are not limited to, contact with parents, detentions, verbal reminders, review of expectations, or a written work assignment with a learning component.

Ongoing interventions may be necessary to sustain and promote positive student behaviour and/or address underlying causes of inappropriate behaviour. For example, ongoing interventions may include, but are not limited to, meetings with parents, volunteer service to the school community, conflict mediation, peer mentoring, and/or a referral to counselling.

Strategies for Addressing Inappropriate Behaviour

When inappropriate behaviour occurs, schools should utilize a range of interventions, supports, and consequences that are developmentally appropriate, and should include opportunities for students to focus on improving behaviour. Consequences for inappropriate behaviour may include, but are not limited to, meeting with the parent(s), student, and principal;[8] referral to a community agency[9] for anger management or substance abuse; and detentions or loss of privileges.

In considering the most appropriate response to address inappropriate behaviour, the following should be taken into consideration:

the particular student and circumstances (e.g., mitigating or other factors)

the nature and severity of the behaviour

the impact on the school climate (i.e., the relationships within the school community)

School Board Policies On Progressive Discipline

Policy Development

In developing their policies on progressive discipline, boards have the flexibility to take into account local needs and circumstances, such as geographical considerations, demographics, cultural needs, and availability of board and community supports and resources.

Boards should draw upon evidence-based practices that promote positive student behaviour. In developing their policies, boards must consult with school councils. They should also consult with parents, principals, teachers, students, their Parent Involvement Committee, their Special Education Advisory Committee, community partners, social service agencies, members of Aboriginal communities (e.g., Elders), and those groups that are traditionally not consulted.

Boards must take into account the needs of individual students by showing sensitivity to diversity, to cultural needs, and to special education needs in their policies, in keeping with the relevant ministry policies on antiracism and ethnocultural equity and antidiscrimination education and with the principles in the ministry document *Ontario First Nation, Métis, and Inuit Education Policy Framework, 2007*. Where possible, the policies should incorporate other relevant board-wide policies, strategies, and initiatives, such as those related to Student Success and character development.

Boards are required to adhere to the Municipal Freedom of Information and Protection of Privacy Act, the Ontario Human Rights Code, and the Education Act and regulations made under the Act in the development and implementation of their policies. Board policies must respect all applicable collective agreements. Boards should consult with their legal counsel and freedom of information coordinators to ensure that they are fulfilling their legal responsibilities.

Policy Components and Implementation Strategies

1. Policy Statement

Board policies on progressive discipline must include the following statements:

> The goal of the policy is to support a safe learning and teaching environment in which every student can reach his or her full potential.

> Appropriate action must consistently be taken to address behaviours that are contrary to provincial and board codes of conduct.

> Progressive discipline is an approach that makes use of a continuum of interventions, supports, and consequences, building upon strategies that promote positive behaviours.

> The range of interventions, supports, and consequences used by the board and all schools must be clear and developmentally appropriate, and must include learning opportunities for students in order to reinforce positive behaviours and help students make good choices.

> For students with special education needs, interventions, supports, and consequences must be consistent with the expectations in the student's IEP.

> The board, and school administrators, must consider all mitigating and other factors, as required by the Education Act and as set out in Ontario Regulation 472/07.

2. Progressive Discipline Implementation Strategy

In developing their progressive discipline policies, boards must incorporate the following procedures as part of their implementation strategy. Boards must:

> require schools to develop and implement a school-wide progressive discipline policy that is consistent with the board's policy;
>
> outline a range of interventions, supports, and consequences, including circumstances in which short-term suspension, long-term suspension, or expulsion may be the response required;
>
> require schools to use the most appropriate response, as outlined in the board's or school's progressive discipline policy, to respond to a student's behaviour. For students with special education needs, interventions, consequences, and supports must be consistent with the expectations in the student's IEP;
>
> develop a process for building on existing partnerships and for developing new partnerships with community agencies, including local police services, to support students and their families;
>
> provide for ongoing dialogue with parents on student achievement and behaviour;
>
> provide opportunities for students to improve the school climate through assuming leadership roles (e.g., peer mediation, mentorship);
>
> review the board's code of conduct to ensure that it is aligned with a progressive discipline approach.

3. Building Partnerships

Policies and programs that promote a positive school environment and support the progressive discipline continuum should be developed and established by building positive relationships that engage the whole school community and its partners. Linkages and coordination among boards, local schools, and community agencies should be established. Through outreach, partnerships already in place may be enhanced and new partnerships with community agencies and members of the community (e.g., Aboriginal Elders) may also be created.

Community agencies are resources that boards can use to deliver prevention or intervention programs (e.g., early and ongoing intervention strategies). Protocols between boards and community agencies are effective ways to establish linkages and to formalize the relationship between them. These protocols facilitate the delivery of prevention and intervention programs, the use of referral processes, and the provision of services and support for students and their parents and families. Where such protocols already exist, they should be reviewed, and where they do not, protocols should be developed to increase the board's capacity to respond to the needs of students. These partnerships must respect collective agreements.

Boards should, wherever possible, collaborate to provide coordinated prevention and intervention programs and services and, where possible, share effective practices.

4. Training Strategy for Administrators, Teachers, and Other School Staff

Boards must put in place a training strategy for all administrators and teachers, including educational assistants, on the board's policy on progressive discipline.

A board should make sure that others are aware of the board's policy on progressive discipline -- for example, school secretaries and custodians, parents, volunteers, community agencies, and school bus operators/drivers.

The training must address the fact that building a supportive learning environment through appropriate interactions between all members of the school community is the responsibility of all staff.

Boards should support ongoing training for teachers and administrators through such opportunities as new-teacher induction programs and e-learning to create and sustain a safe teaching and learning environment.

5. Communication Strategy

For a progressive discipline approach to be effective, it is important that all members of the school community, including teachers, students, and parents, understand and support the progressive discipline approach. Boards must actively communicate policies and procedures to all students, parents, staff members, and school council members. Boards should share this information, as appropriate, with parents whose first language is a language other than English or French.

6. Monitoring and Review

Boards must establish performance indicators for monitoring, reviewing, and evaluating the effectiveness of board policies and procedures. These indicators should be developed in consultation with teachers, students, parents, school councils, their Special Education Advisory Committee, their Parent Involvement Committee, and service providers in the community. Boards will also conduct a cyclical review of their policies and procedures in a timely manner. This review may include an analysis of school climate by their schools on a regular cycle, as determined by the board.

Appendix: Excerpts From The Legislation

Education Act, as amended by the Education Amendment Act (Progressive Discipline and School Safety), 2007

Relevant excerpts from sections 301, 306, and 310 of the Education Act, as amended by the Education Amendment Act (Progressive Discipline and School Safety), 2007, are provided below for ease of reference.

Policies and guidelines governing discipline

301. (6) The Minister may establish policies and guidelines with respect to disciplining pupils, specifying, for example, the circumstances in which a pupil is subject to discipline and the forms and the extent of discipline that may be imposed in particular circumstances.

Duty of boards

(9) The Minister may require boards to comply with policies and guidelines established under this section.

Suspension

Activities leading to possible suspension

306. (1) A principal shall consider whether to suspend a pupil if he or she believes that the pupil has engaged in any of the following activities while at school, at a school-related activity or in other circumstances where engaging in the activity will have an impact on the school climate:

1. Uttering a threat to inflict serious bodily harm on another person.
2. Possessing alcohol or illegal drugs.
3. Being under the influence of alcohol.
4. Swearing at a teacher or at another person in a position of authority.
5. Committing an act of vandalism that causes extensive damage to school property at the pupil's school or to property located on the premises of the pupil's school.
6. Bullying.
7. Any other activity that is an activity for which a principal may suspend a pupil under a policy of the board.

Factors principal must consider

(2) In considering whether to suspend a pupil for engaging in an activity described in subsection (1), a principal shall take into account any mitigating or other factors prescribed by the regulations.

Suspension, Investigation And Possible Expulsion

Activities leading to suspension

310. (1) A principal shall suspend a pupil if he or she believes that the pupil has engaged in any of the following activities while at school, at a school-related activity or in other circumstances where engaging in the activity will have an impact on the school climate:

1. Possessing a weapon, including possessing a firearm.

2. Using a weapon to cause or to threaten bodily harm to another person.
3. Committing physical assault on another person that causes bodily harm requiring treatment by a medical practitioner.
4. Committing sexual assault.
5. Trafficking in weapons or in illegal drugs.
6. Committing robbery.
7. Giving alcohol to a minor.
8. Any other activity that, under a policy of a board, is an activity for which a principal must suspend a pupil and, therefore in accordance with this Part, conduct an investigation to determine whether to recommend to the board that the pupil be expelled.

Same

(2) A pupil who is suspended under this section is suspended from his or her school and from engaging in all school-related activities.

Duration of suspension

(3) A principal may suspend a pupil under this section for up to 20 school days and, in considering how long the suspension should be, the principal shall take into account any mitigating or other factors prescribed by the regulations.

Assignment to program, etc.

(4) When a principal suspends a pupil under this section, he or she shall assign the pupil to a program for suspended pupils in accordance with any policies or guidelines issued by the Minister.

Ontario Regulation 472/07, "Suspension and Expulsion of Pupils"

Relevant excerpts from Ontario Regulation 472/07, made under the Education Act, are provided below for ease of reference.

Mitigating factors

2. For the purposes of subsections 306 (2), 306 (4), 310 (3), 311.1 (4) and clauses 311.3 (7) (b) and 311.4 (2) (b) of the Act, the following mitigating factors shall be taken into account:

1. The pupil does not have the ability to control his or her behaviour.
2. The pupil does not have the ability to understand the foreseeable consequences of his or her behaviour.
3. The pupil's continuing presence in the school does not create an unacceptable risk to the safety of any person.

Other factors

3. For the purposes of subsections 306 (2), 306 (4), 310 (3), 311.1 (4) and clauses 311.3 (7) (b) and 311.4 (2) (b) of the Act, the following other factors shall be taken into account if they would mitigate the seriousness of the activity for which the pupil may be or is being suspended or expelled:

1. The pupil's history.
2. Whether a progressive discipline approach has been used with the pupil.
3. Whether the activity for which the pupil may be or is being suspended or expelled was related to any harassment of the pupil because of his or her race, ethnic origin, religion, disability, gender or sexual orientation or to any other harassment.
4. How the suspension or expulsion would affect the pupil's ongoing education.
5. The age of the pupil.
6. In the case of a pupil for whom an individual education plan has been developed,
    i. whether the behaviour was a manifestation of a disability identified in the pupil's individual education plan,
    ii. whether appropriate individualized accommodation has been provided, and
    iii. whether the suspension or expulsion is likely to result in an aggravation or worsening of the pupil's behaviour or conduct.

1. The term *student*, as used in this memorandum, refers to *pupil*, as used in the Education Act.
2. In this memorandum, *school board(s)* and *board(s)* refer to district school boards and school authorities.
3. Policy/Program Memorandum No. 141, "School Board Programs for Students on Long-Term Suspension", August 23, 2007, and Policy/Program Memorandum No. 142, "School Board Programs for Expelled Students", August 23, 2007.
4. Policy/Program Memorandum No. 144, "Bullying Prevention and Intervention", October 4, 2007.
5. *Safe Schools Policy and Practice: An Agenda for Action*, Report of the Safe Schools Action Team (Toronto: June 2006), p. 24.
6. *Safe Schools Policy and Practice: An Agenda for Action*, Report of the Safe Schools Action Team (Toronto: June 2006), p. 6.
7. In this memorandum, *parent(s)* refers to parent(s) and guardian(s). Parental involvement applies, except in cases where the student is eighteen years of age or over or is sixteen or seventeen years of age and has "withdrawn from parental control".
8. In this memorandum, *principal* refers to the principal or to a person designated by the principal or by the board.
9. Community agencies include a range of community service agencies, local organizations, and programs.

APPENDIX F

Summary of *S.J. v. Toronto Catholic District School Board*

In the 2006 decision of *S.J. v. Toronto Catholic District School Board*,[1] the Ontario Divisional Court upheld the decision of a principal to impose a limited expulsion of an 11-year old student for bringing a pen-knife to school and threatening pupils. This decision demonstrates the courts' tendency to show deference toward the decisions of administrators and the courts' recognition of the importance of maintaining a safe school and the need for administrators to act quickly to protect students. The Divisional Court found that in addition to the principal's conduct not being patently unreasonable, it was "little short of impeccable." As a result, this decision provides helpful guidance for administrators as an example of how to properly conduct an investigation, and we provide herein a detailed chronology of the steps taken in the investigation.

The Facts

To provide some insight into this decision, the following are the detailed steps taken by the principal in his inquiry, which lead to the limited expulsion:

- ❑ The principal learned of the incident when a teacher gave the knife in question to him (having been given the knife by the two female victims) and reported the allegations of the threat made by the victims.

- ❑ He interviewed the girls separately and believed that their stories had a ring of truth.

- ❑ He spoke to two teachers on yard duty, who were unaware of the incident.

- ❑ He interviewed the accused pupil in the presence of his teacher. Initially the pupil denied knowing anything about the knife. The principal then stepped into the class and asked whose pen he was holding, and the students identified it as belonging to the pupil. When the principal asked if there was anything special about the pen, a

---

[1] [2006] O.J. No. 2878, 214 O.A.C. 39, 50 Admin. L.R. (4th) 243, 143 C.R.R. (2d) 170, 150 A.C.W.S. (3d) 83 (Ont. S.C.J.); supp. [2006] O.J. No. 3902, 216 O.A.C. 204, 50 Admin. L.R. (4th) 261, 152 A.C.W.S. (3d) 42 (Ont. Div. Ct.).

student replied that "there's a knife inside it." At that point, the pupil acknowledged his initial falsehood and explained that he got the knife from his cousin.

❑ The principal concluded that the pupil had brought a concealed pen knife to school and he had not been initially truthful and it was necessary to isolate him because of the threat of violence.

❑ The principal contacted his superintendent and the police, since a weapon was involved and arranged for the victims to write their statements separately.

❑ A police officer arrived and took statements from the accused and the two victims.

❑ The principal prepared a "Notice of Suspension Pending Expulsion" and the Police Officer delivered the accused home with the notice.

❑ To continue his inquiry, the principal spoke with the accused's mother three times that afternoon, and as a result, he interviewed the accused's friend (who said he saw nothing happen). He told the mother that if the facts were as serious as they appeared, her son would likely be facing a limited expulsion.

❑ On the following Monday, the accused's mother told the principal the name of another witness who would apparently say that he did not hear or see any threatening behaviour. The principal interviewed this witness, whose report did not match what the mother had indicated.

❑ The principal finished his inquiry on the Monday and decided to impose a one-year limited expulsion on the accused, setting out his reasons in his "principal's inquiry".

❑ The evidence and documentation revealed that he considered the accused's special needs and considered the accused's increasingly aggressive behaviour throughout the year when deciding that a limited expulsion was appropriate. The principal also considered whether there were any mitigating circumstances, concluding that the accused showed the ability to control his behaviour and to foresee the consequences of his behaviour and that his continued presence created an unacceptable risk to the students.

❑ The principal imposed a limited expulsion from April 8, 2002 to March 21, 2003. He advised the mother of a possible alternate placement in the language impaired class at another school and provided the opportunity for his immediate transfer, which the mother eventually accepted.

The Decision

The Divisional Court held that the principal did not deny procedural fairness to the accused, and that the actions of the principal were scrupulously fair, reasoned and appropriate. The Court noted that the principal conducted himself "as we imagine most parents with children at Sacred Heart would hope a principal would — with respect for the rights of A.A. and the rights of other children at the school."[2] The Court summarized the principal's actions as follows:

> He conducted an investigation of the incident by talking to all the students involved, including those identified by Ms. S.J.; he put the allegations to A.A. and obtained his response; he spoke with Ms. S.J. several times and kept her informed; he reviewed A.A.'s history of behavioural problems; he canvassed the mitigating factors set out in O. Reg. 37/01 and decided there were none; he took into account the students' knowledge that A.A. had brought a knife to school.[3]

The Court also rejected allegations that the school board's appeal process regarding the limited expulsion constituted a denial of procedural fairness. There was no obligation to conduct a *de novo* hearing for the appeal (*i.e.*, a fresh hearing of all of the evidence). The fact that the accused was required to present first was not unfair. It was not unfair that the victims were not called as witnesses, nor that hearsay was admitted. The Court upheld the school board's decision not to admit the student records of the victims in the appeal on the basis that their contents were irrelevant.

In respect of the school board's appeal, the Court did find that the reasons of the board regarding its disposition of the appeal fell "dangerously close to being inadequate."[4] The board dismissed the parent's appeal, and stated that it was satisfied that the principal considered all relevant factors in arriving at his decision. The Court cautioned that the board should be made aware of the importance of giving adequate reasons of any of its decisions.

The Court also rejected the accused's allegations that the board violated the pupil and his mother's rights to liberty and security of the person under section 7 of the *Charter*.

---

[2] *Ibid.*, at para. 39.
[3] *Ibid.*, at para. 38.
[4] *Ibid.*, at para. 54.

APPENDIX G

Summary of K.B.(Litigation Guardian of) v. Toronto District School Board

In January of 2008, the Ontario Divisional Court upheld a principal's decision to transfer two pupils based on safety concerns. The Court confirmed that a pupil has no right to attend at a particular school, and that in these circumstances, a school board has the power to transfer a pupil.

The Facts

- The two students in question (K.B. and T.M.) were involved in an incident (with two other students) wherein a fifth student was assaulted and thrown into the window of a school door.
- The investigation revealed at least one previous incident, wherein K.B. had threatened the victim.
- The principal suspended K.B. and T.M. for 16 days each, and decided to transfer the pupils due to safety concerns for individuals at the school such as the victim and witnesses.
- One of the pupils was precluded from attending at the school due to bail conditions imposed in respect of the incident.
- Subsequently, the pupils were advised that they were being denied access to the school, due to concerns regarding the safety of the victim.

The Decision

The Divisional Court held that the principal had the power to deny the pupils access to the school, based on the principal's view that their presence would endanger the safety of the victim and other students. The Court further found that although a transfer was a potentially serious disruption for a student, it was a lesser consequence than an expulsion.[1]

The Court held that the power to transfer students in these circumstances is implicit in the powers of a school board. The Court noted that the Principal

---

[1] This court noted that this was recognized in s. 8(f) of the settlement reached between the OHRC and the Toronto District School Board in October 28, 2005.

concluded that there was a need to transfer the students for safety reasons and noted that this school was not the designated school for either of the students.

The Court also held that the only factor to be considered in deciding whether to deny a person access to school premises was whether the individual's presence is detrimental to the safety or well-being of a person on the school premises, and that there was no reference to the interests of the person who may be excluded. In any event; however, the Court concluded that the Principal considered the best interests of all of the students, not only the best interests of the applicants.

The Court found that there was no breach of the duty of procedural fairness by the principal. He conducted an investigation before deciding to transfer the pupils. He invited the students to give their side of the story, although they refused on the advice of counsel. There was also evidence that the pupils knew the allegations against them. The principal provided notice of the transfer and adequate reasons for the transfer.

The Divisional Court also rejected the applicants' arguments that their s. 7 *Charter* rights to liberty and security of the person or their section 15 *Charter* rights to equality were breached.

INDEX

ACCESS
access to school premises
(Regulation), 79-80
denial of access
- generally, 43-44
- removal of application to pupils, 44
- students with special needs, 45-46

Education Act provisions, 55

ACTIVITIES LEADING TO POSSIBLE SUSPENSION, 15-16, 55-56

APPEAL
expulsion
- decision of tribunal, 38
- *Education Act* provisions, 67-68
- generally, 36
- hearing of appeal, 37
- Ministry regulations, 38
- notice of appeal, 36-37
- parties, 37
- powers of designated tribunal, 37-38
- who may appeal, 36

notice of appeal
- expulsion, 36-37
- regulations, 82

regulations
- hearing of appeal, 82-83
- notice of appeal, 82

suspensions
- board committee, 23-24
- *Education Act* provisions, 57-59, 64
- initial suspension, where no expulsion, 31, 34-35
- notice of appeal, 23
- one-day suspensions, 21
- optional suspension review process, 23
- parties to suspension appeal, 24
- powers of board committee, 25
- removal for less than a day, 21
- student's right to attend, 24
- suspension appeal hearing process, 23-24
- time periods, revisions to, 7
- who may appeal, 23

ASSIGNMENT OF EXPELLED PUPIL, 35, 41-42

BALANCE OF PROBABILITIES, 16

BOARD EXPULSION, 6, 40, 42

BULLYING, *see also* POLICY/PROGRAM MEMORANDUM 144
as activity for suspension, 5
cyber-bullying, 5, 20
definition, 16-18, 137-138
generally, 16
positive school climate, 18
power imbalances, 17
school board policies, 18-20

CASE SUMMARIES
K.B. (Litigation Guardian of) v. Toronto District School Board, 165-166
S.J. v. Toronto Catholic District School Board, 161-163

CHILD AND FAMILY SERVICES REVIEW BOARD, 36-38, 82

CLOSING EXERCISES, 54-55

CO-INSTRUCTIONAL ACTIVITIES, 76-77

CODE OF CONDUCT, *see also* POLICY/PROGRAM MEMORANDUM 128
Education Act provisions, 51-52
generally, 7-8

COMMUNICABLE DISEASES, 76

COMMUNICATION STRATEGY, 154-155

COMMUNITY PARTNERS, 95

CREDIBILITY OF WITNESSES, 29

CYBER-BULLYING, 5, 20

DENIAL OF ACCESS
generally, 43-44
removal of application to pupils, 44
students with special needs, 45-46

DISCIPLINE, *see also* EXPULSION; POLICY/PROGRAM MEMORANDUM 145; SUSPENSIONS
discretionary discipline, 4
mandatory discipline, 4
off-school property conduct, 20
progressive discipline
- application of, 5
- definition, 12
- generally, 11
- intervention strategies, 12-13
- policies, 12-14
- requirement of, 11
- students with special needs, 14-15
students with special needs, 46-47

DISCIPLINE COMMITTEES, 7

DISCRETIONARY DISCIPLINE, 4

DURATION OF SUSPENSIONS, 21

EARLY INTERVENTION STRATEGIES, 12-13

EDUCATION ACT, *see also* EDUCATION ACT PROVISIONS
denial of access
- generally, 43-44
- removal of application to pupils, 44
- students with special needs, 45-46
expulsion appeals, 36
expulsions, 25-26
suspensions, 15
EDUCATION ACT PROVISIONS, *see also* REGULATIONS
access to school premises, 55
board policies and guidelines governing conduct, 52-54
duties of principal, 75-77
excerpts of legislation
- Policy/Program Memorandum 128, 96-98
- Policy/Program Memorandum 141, 106-113
- Policy/Program Memorandum 142, 124-133
- Policy/Program Memorandum 144, 142-144
- Policy/Program Memorandum 145, 155-158
interpretation, 51
opening and closing exercises, 54-55
provincial code of conduct, 51-52
regulations, 73-74
suspension
- activities leading to possible suspension, 55-56
- appeal of suspension, 57-59
- notice of suspension, 56-57
- one suspension per occurrence, 56

EDUCATION ACT — *cont'd*
suspension, investigation and possible expulsion
- activities leading to suspension, 59-60
- appeal of expulsion, 67-68
- appeal of suspension, 64
- expulsion hearing, 64-65
- expulsions under old Part XIII, 72
- full expulsion, 72
- if expulsion not recommended, 62
- if expulsion recommended, 62-63
- if pupil expelled, 66
- if pupil not expelled, 65-66
- investigation following suspension, 61-63
- limited expulsion, 72
- new Part XIII applies, 72
- notice of expulsion, 66-67
- old Part XIII applies, 71
- personal information, 73
- powers of other board, 69-70
- resident pupils, 71
- return to school after expulsion, 70
- status of expelled pupil, 69
- successful completion of program, 70

transitional provisions, 71
transitional regulations, 73

EDUCATION AMENDMENT ACT, 2007
introduction to changes, 3-4
transitional provisions
- full expulsions, 43
- generally, 43
- limited expulsions, 43

EDUCATION OF SUSPENDED AND EXPELLED PUPILS, *see also* POLICY/PROGRAM MEMORANDUM 141; POLICY/PROGRAM MEMORANDUM 142
board policies, 39-40

Education Act provisions, 68-69
generally, 7
long-term suspension or expulsion, 40-41
overview, 39
pending expulsion, 27
short-term suspension, 40
Student Action Plan, 41

EXPULSION, *see also* EDUCATION OF SUSPENDED AND EXPELLED PUPILS
appeal process
- decision of tribunal, 38
- generally, 36
- hearing of appeal, 37
- Ministry regulations, 38
- notice of appeal, 36-37
- parties, 37
- powers of designated tribunal, 37-38
- who may appeal, 36

board expulsion, 6, 40, 42
duration of suspension pending possible expulsion, 26-27
Education Act provisions
- activities leading to suspension, 59-60
- appeal of expulsion, 67-68
- education of expelled pupils, 68-69
- expulsion hearing, 64-65
- expulsions under old Part XIII, 72
- full expulsion, 72
- if expulsion not recommended, 62
- if expulsion recommended, 62-63
- if pupil expelled, 66
- if pupil not expelled, 65-66
- investigation following suspension, 61-63
- limited expulsion, 72
- new Part XIII applies, 72
- notice of suspension, 60-61
- old Part XIII applies, 71
- personal information, 73
- powers of other board, 69-70

EXPULSION — *cont'd*
- programs for suspended, expelled pupils, 68-69
- regulations, 73-74
- resident pupils, 71
- return to school after expulsion, 70
- status of expelled pupil, 69
- successful completion of program, 70
- transitional provisions, 71
- transitional regulations, 73

Education Act regulations, 81-83
expulsion hearing
- board committee requirements, 33
- decision of board committee, 34
- generally, 33
- parties, 33
- submissions, 34

investigation
- generally, 28
- tips for conduct of investigation, 29-30

limited expulsions, 72
listed activities, 26
mitigating or other factors, 30
notice of suspension, 27-28, 30-31, 31-32
overview, 25-26
principals, power of, 6
principals and, 6
Re-Entry Process, 41
regulations, 81-83
return to school after completion of program, 41-42
school boards
- board expulsion, 6
- school expulsion, 6

school expulsion, 6, 42
steps where expulsion not recommended
- appeal of initial suspension, 31
- review of initial suspension, 30
- written notice, 30-31

steps where expulsion recommended
- board committee requirements, 33
- decision of board committee, 34
- expulsion hearing, 33
- parties to expulsion hearing, 33
- report regarding recommendation, 31
- response to report, 32
- submissions to expulsion hearing, 34
- written notice, 31-32

steps where pupil is expelled
- assignment of expelled pupil, 35
- written notice of board committee decisions, 35-36

steps where pupil not expelled
- appeal of initial suspension, 34-35
- written notice of board committee decisions, 35

Student Action Plan, 41
transition provisions
- full expulsions, 43
- limited expulsions, 43

EXPULSION HEARING
board committee requirements, 33
conduct of, 7
decision of board committee, 34
generally, 33
parties, 33
submissions, 34

FORMS, 22

FULL EXPULSION, 72

HEARINGS
appeals
- expulsion appeal, 37
- regulations, 82-83
- suspension appeal, 23-24

expulsion hearing
- conduct of, 7
- decision of board committee, 34
- *Education Act* provisions, 64-65
- generally, 33
- parties, 33

INDEX

HEARINGS — *cont'd*
- submissions, 34

HUMAN RIGHTS
and mitigating factors, 5, 10
potential of increase in complaints, 10
students with special needs
- mitigating factors, application of, 10-11
- progressive discipline, 14

INDIVIDUAL EDUCATION PLAN (IEP), 14

INFRACTIONS, 4, 16. S*ee also* EXPULSION; SUSPENSIONS

INTERVENTION STRATEGIES, 12-13, 150

INVESTIGATION
credibility of witnesses, 29
Education Act provisions
- activities leading to suspension, 59-60
- if expulsion not recommended, 62
- if expulsion recommended, 62-63
- investigation following suspension, 61-63
- notice of suspension, 60-61
generally, 28
tips for conduct of investigation, 29-30

K.B. (LITIGATION GUARDIAN OF) V. TORONTO DISTRICT SCHOOL BOARD, 165-166

LIMITED EXPULSIONS, 43, 72

LONG-TERM SUSPENSIONS, 40-41, 102-103

MANDATORY DISCIPLINE, 4

MITIGATING FACTORS
application of factors, 9-10
consideration of, 4
expansion of, 5
expulsion, 30
vs. "other factors," 9
overview, 8-9
regulations, 81
students with special needs, 10-11
suspension, 21

NOTICES
notice of appeal
- expulsions, 36-37
- regulations, 82
- suspensions, 23
notice of board committee decisions
- where pupil is expelled, 35
- where pupil not expelled, 35
notice of suspension
- *Education Act* provisions, 56-57, 60-61
- generally, 22
- where expulsion not recommended, 27-28
- where expulsion recommended, 30-31

OFF-SCHOOL PROPERTY CONDUCT
cyber-bullying, 5, 20
discipline for, 5
generally, 20

ONE-DAY SUSPENSIONS, 21

ONGOING INTERVENTION STRATEGIES, 12-13

OPENING EXERCISES, 54-55

OPTIONAL SUSPENSION REVIEW PROCESS, 23

"OTHER FACTORS"
expulsion, 30
generally, 9
vs. mitigating factors, 9-10

"OTHER FACTORS" — *cont'd*
regulations, 81-82
suspension, 21

OUTREACH PROGRAMS, 95

PARENTS
roles and responsibilities, 95

PERSONAL INFORMATION, 73

PLANNING MEETING, 41, 105, 121-122

POLICE, 95

POLICY/PROGRAM MEMORANDUM 128
excerpts from legislation, 96-98
generally, 7
introduction, 87-89
provincial code of conduct
- purposes of the code, 90-91
- roles and responsibilities
-- community partners and police, 95
-- parents, 95
-- principals, 93-94
-- school boards, 92-93
-- students, 94
-- teachers and other school staff members, 94
- standards of behaviour
-- respect, civility, and responsible citizenship, 91-92
-- safety, 91-92
requirements for school boards
- development or revision of local codes of conduct, 89-90
- generally, 89
- revision of school board codes of conduct, 89-90

POLICY/PROGRAM MEMORANDUM 141
accountability and reporting requirements, 106

board policies, 39-40
education under long-term suspension or expulsion, 40-41
education under short-term suspension, 40
excerpts from legislation, 106-113
general requirements
- considerations for program development, 100-101
- generally, 100
- school board policies on program operation, 101
generally, 7
introduction, 99-100
overview, 39
planning meeting, 105
program delivery, 105-106
program requirements
- academic component, 103
- generally, 102
- long-term suspension, 102-103
- non-academic component, 103-104
- Student Action Plan, 102, 104
- students suspended from eleven to twenty school days, 102-103
- students suspended from six to ten school days, 102
re-entry meeting, 105

POLICY/PROGRAM MEMORANDUM 142
accountability and reporting requirements, 123-124
board policies, 39-40
excerpts from legislation, 124-133
general requirements
- considerations for program development, 118
- expulsion, 117
- school board policies on program operation, 118-119
- suspension pending expulsion, 117
generally, 7
introduction, 115-116

POLICY/PROGRAM

MEMORANDUM 142 — *cont'd*
overview, 39
planning meeting, 121-122
program delivery, 123
program requirements
- academic component, 119
- components of programs for expelled students, 119
- non-academic component, 120
- Student Action Plan, 120

re-entry plan, 122-123
Student Action Plan, 120, 122

POLICY/PROGRAM MEMORANDUM 144
bullying, defined, 16-18, 137-138
excerpts from legislation, 142-144
generally, 16
introduction, 135-136
positive school climate, 18
power imbalances, 17
research, 137
safe schools teams, 141
school board policies on bullying
- generally, 18-20
- policy components and implementation strategies
  - communication and outreach strategies, 140
  - definition of bullying, 139
  - intervention strategies, 139-140
  - monitoring and review, 141
  - policy statement, 139
  - prevention strategies, 139
  - training strategies for community members, 140
- policy development, 138

school-level plans, 141

POLICY/PROGRAM MEMORANDUM 145
background, 148
excerpts from legislation, 155-158
generally, 11
intervention strategies, 12-13, 150
introduction, 147

positive student behaviour
- generally, 149
- prevention, 149

progressive discipline, defined, 12
progressive discipline approach
- early and ongoing intervention strategies, 150
- generally, 150
- strategies for addressing inappropriate behaviour, 151

progressive discipline policies, 12-14
responses to inappropriate behaviour, 13
school board policies on progressive discipline
policy components and implementation strategies
- building partnerships, 153-154
- communication strategy, 154
- monitoring and review, 155
- policy statement, 152
- progressive discipline implementation strategy, 153
- training strategy for school staff, 154
- policy development, 151-152

students with special needs, 14-15

POSITIVE SCHOOL CLIMATE, 18, 136

POWER IMBALANCES, 17

PREVENTION, 149

PRINCIPALS, *see also* EXPULSION; SUSPENSIONS
credibility of witnesses, assessment of, 29
denial of access, 43-46
duties of principal (*Education Act* provisions), 75-77
expulsion, power of, 6
roles and responsibilities, 93-94

PROGRESSIVE DISCIPLINE, *see also* POLICY/PROGRAM MEMORANDUM 145
application of, 5
definition, 12
generally, 11
intervention strategies, 12-13
policies, 12-14
requirement of, 11
students with special needs, 14-15

PROVINCIAL CODE OF CONDUCT. *See* CODE OF CONDUCT; POLICY/PROGRAM MEMORANDUM 128

RE-ENTRY MEETING, 105

RE-ENTRY PLAN, 122-123

RE-ENTRY PROCESS, 41

REGULATIONS
access to school premises, 79-80
appeal hearing, 82-83
expulsion appeal regulations, 38
under Part XIII, 74
personal information, 73
suspension and expulsion of students, 81-83
transitional regulations, 73

RESIDENT PUPILS, 71

RESPONSES TO INAPPROPRIATE BEHAVIOUR, 13

RETURN TO SCHOOL, 41-42, 70

SAFE SCHOOLS ACT, 3

SAFE SCHOOLS TEAMS, 141

SAFETY ISSUES, 46, 91-92

SCHOOL BOARDS, *see also* POLICY/PROGRAM MEMORANDUM 128; POLICY/PROGRAM MEMORANDUM 141; POLICY/PROGRAM MEMORANDUM 142; POLICY/PROGRAM MEMORANDUM 144; POLICY/PROGRAM MEMORANDUM 145
bullying, policies on, 18-20
early intervention strategies, 12-13
education of suspended and expelled pupils, 39-40
expulsion
- board expulsion, 6
- school expulsion, 6
policies and guidelines governing conduct, 52-54
powers of other board, 69-70
roles and responsibilities, 92-93
suspension appeal policy, 24

SCHOOL EXPULSION, 6, 42

S.J. V. TORONTO CATHOLIC DISTRICT SCHOOL BOARD, 161-163

SPECIAL NEEDS. *See* STUDENTS WITH SPECIAL NEEDS

STAFF MEMBERS
roles and responsibilities, 94
training strategies, 154

STATUS OF EXPELLED PUPIL, 69

STUDENT ACTION PLAN, 41, 102, 104, 120, 122

STUDENT DISCIPLINE REGIME
education of suspended and expelled pupils, 39
expulsion

STUDENT DISCIPLINE REGIME
— *cont'd*
- duration of suspension pending possible expulsion, 26-27
- education for pupils suspended pending expulsion, 27
- investigation, 28-30
- mitigating or other factors, 30
- notice of suspension, 27-28
- overview, 25-26
- steps where expulsion not recommended, 30-31

introduction, 3-4

mitigating factors
- application of factors, 9-10
- overview, 8-9
- students with special needs, 10-11

overview of changes
- bullying, 5
- code of conduct, 7-8
- discipline committees, composition of, 7
- education for suspended and expelled pupils, 7
- mandatory discipline, 4
- mitigating factors and progressive discipline, 5
- off-school property conduct, 5
- principal expulsions, removal of, 6
- teacher suspensions, removal of, 6
- time periods, revisions to, 7

progressive discipline
- definition, 12
- generally, 11
- policies, 12-14
- students with special needs, 14-15

suspensions
- appeal process, 23-25
- bullying, 16-20
- completion of forms, 22
- duration, 21
- interpretation of listed activities, 16
- mitigating and other factors, 21
- notice of suspension, 22
- off-school property conduct, 20
- overview, 15

STUDENTS, *see also* EXPULSION; HUMAN RIGHTS; SUSPENSIONS
appeal, attendance at, 24
resident pupils, 71
return to school, 41-42
roles and responsibilities, 94

STUDENTS WITH SPECIAL NEEDS
denial of access provisions, 45-46
discipline, 46-47
mitigating factors, application of, 10-11
progressive discipline, 14-15
safety issues, 46

SUCCESSFUL COMPLETION OF PROGRAM, 70

SUSPENSION FORM, 22

SUSPENSIONS, *see also* EDUCATION OF SUSPENDED AND EXPELLED PUPILS; EXPULSION
activities leading to possible suspension, 15-16, 55-56
appeal
- board committee, 23-24
- initial suspension, where no expulsion, 31, 34-35
- notice of appeal, 23
- one-day suspensions, 21
- optional suspension review process, 23
- parties to suspension appeal, 24
- powers of board committee, 25
- removal for less than a day, 21
- student's right to attend, 24
- suspension appeal hearing process, 23-24
- time periods, revisions to, 7

SUSPENSIONS — *cont'd*
- who may appeal, 23

bullying
- as activity for suspension, 5
- cyber-bullying, 5
- definition, 16-18
- generally, 16
- positive school climate, 18
- power imbalances, 17
- school board policies, 18-20

completion of forms, 22
duration, 21
duration, pending expulsion, 26-27
Education Act provisions
- activities leading to possible suspension, 55-56
- appeal of suspension, 57-59
- education of suspended pupils, 68-69
- notice of suspension, 56-57, 60-61
- one suspension per occurrence, 56

Education Act regulations, 81-83
from eleven to twenty school days, 102-103
interpretation of listed activities, 16
less than one day, 21
long-term suspensions, 40-41, 102-103
mitigating factors, 21
notice of suspension
- generally, 22
- where expulsion not recommended, 27-28
- where expulsion recommended, 30-31

off-school property conduct
- cyber-bullying, 5, 20
- discipline for, 5
- generally, 20

one-day suspensions, 21
"other factors," 21
overview, 15
regulations, 81-83
review of initial suspension, 30
for same occurrence, 21
from six to ten school days, 102
teacher suspensions, removal of, 6

TEACHERS
roles and responsibilities, 94
suspensions by, 6

TRAINING STRATEGIES, 154

TRANSITIONAL PROVISIONS
full expulsions, 43
generally, 43
limited expulsions, 43
regulations, 73

VIOLENT INCIDENT FORM, 22

WITNESSES
credibility of witnesses, 29

ZERO-TOLERANCE APPROACH, 4, 5